D0204253

Congress,
Human Nature,
and the
Federal Debt

Congress, Human Nature, and the Federal Debt

ESSAYS ON THE POLITICAL PSYCHOLOGY OF DEFICIT SPENDING

Cole S. Brembeck

Foreword by James M. Buchanan

PRAEGER

New York
Westport, Connecticut
London

Library of Congress Cataloging-in-Publication Data

Brembeck, Cole Speicher.
  Congress, human nature, and the federal debt : essays on the
political psychology of deficit spending / Cole S. Brembeck ; foreword by James M.
Buchanan.
      p.   cm.
  Includes bibliographical references and index.
  ISBN 0-275-93674-0 (alk. paper)
  1. Debts, Public—United States—Psychological aspects.
  2. Government spending policy—United States—Psychological aspects.
  I. Title.
  HJ8101.B74 1991
  336.3'4'0973—dc20   90-28077

British Library Cataloguing in Publication Data is available.

Library of Congress Catalog Card Number: 90-28077
ISBN: 0-275-93674-0

First published in 1991

Praeger Publishers, One Madison Avenue, New York, NY 10010
An imprint of Greenwood Publishing Group, Inc.

Printed in the United States of America

The paper used in this book complies with the
Permanent Paper Standard issued by the National
Information Standards Organization (Z39.48–1984).

10   9   8   7   6   5   4   3   2   1

To the memory of my father,

a citizen-state legislator, who,

though a stranger to "political psychology,"

taught me enduring lessons about it.

Contents

IV
Will Congress Pay Off the Debt, and If So, How?

V
A Proposal to Ponder

Foreword

We live in an exchange culture, and our economic relationships are based on the central recognition that there are mutual gains from exchange. Most of us provide work to our employers in exchange for money wages or a salary, which we then exchange for consumption goods and services in the market. The economy is a complex network of reciprocal and voluntary exchanges between and among individuals, firms, and associations of individuals. Mutuality of gain is insured by the existence of an exit option available to any and all persons.

This generalized description falls down only in our relationship with government. In what sense do we "exchange" with government? And in what sense can we say that such "exchange" is voluntary? It is naive to think that persons pay taxes "in exchange" for the benefits they receive from governmentally provided services, since the fundamental characteristics of an exchange relationship are missing. Although it remains useful as a normative ideal, any "voluntary exchange theory of taxation" is misleading as a positive theory. We do not pay taxes in some reciprocal exchange for the public service benefits we receive; and we do not get such benefits because we pay taxes. Instead, we pay taxes under the coercive levy of government, and we receive benefits from the gratuitous provision by government. There is no reciprocal or two-sided relationship between taxes and benefits in the fiscal reality that we observe, and this simple fact holds whether or not we live in a democracy.

In democracy, we do, indeed, influence governmental decisions, through the electoral process. Congressmen hold office subject to electoral approval. Coalitions of congressmen, in turn, determine how taxes are to be imposed on us, and how funds are to be expended. Because of the nonreciprocal nature of the fiscal process, each and every one of us seeks to reduce our tax liability, and therefore indirectly, congressmen remain always reluctant to increase taxes beyond some limits. On the other hand, and again because of the nonreciprocal nature of the process, each and every one of us seeks to secure an increase in the benefits from governmental spending programs. More directly, congressmen respond by trying to shift budgetary outlay always higher and higher.

In a simple balanced budget world, the elected politicians would have to do something that imposes pain on constituents, namely, impose taxes, in order to do something that provides pleasure, namely increase program benefits. But in our world, elected politicians are allowed escape from this dilemma through their ability to issue public debt. The issue of public debt (deficit financing) allows elected politicians to refrain from imposing onerous taxes while, at the same time, spending public monies. We should not be at all surprised that the budget deficit emerges as a major problem in modern democracy.

This explanation all seems so simple that it may be difficult to understand how and why it took economists and others so long to recognize it, and how, even now, such explanation is explicitly rejected by so many. The merit of this book is that the author commences from this explanation as the basis for further examination. The book is a set of related essays in post-public choice political psychology.

The ultimate diagnosis of the deficit problem does not offer optimism for effective reform. The modern regime of deficit financing stems from neither error nor evil. A structural problem requires structural reform. We must understand both how politics works and the psychology of how politicians behave before we can think about shoring up the structure of modern democracy.

James M. Buchanan
George Mason University

Preface

First, a word about the relationship of these 14 essays to one another. I would be pleased if I could describe them as companion pieces, linked sequentially in a systematic study of the political psychology of the federal debt. But I cannot, for my purpose was more modest. I thought of myself, rather, as taking an interested scholar's walk around the debt problem and sizing it up from various psychological perspectives. When I came upon one that intrigued me I stopped to investigate and sometimes to write. This subjective approach accounts for my calling the results "essays," rather than "chapters." While they obviously bear a relationship to one another, their closer ties are to the central theme: the human factor in the federal debt.

In spite of their topical natures, however, the essays do group themselves around the five parts indicated in the contents. Because talk of money tends to dominate discussions of the debt, I take some time in Part I to redefine it in terms of human behavior. That view informs the entire book. Part II explores the psychological roots of the debt, and from three quite different perspectives. In Part III the scene shifts more directly to Congress. The five essays in Part III examine the impact of debt on representative government. Part IV confronts the future: Will Congress pay off the debt? The political psychology of debt retirement is examined, and four possible scenarios are discussed. A prediction is ventured. In the final essay I offer an idea to ponder for managing the debt. It is consistent with the political psychology of debt and our democratic tradition.

As with most authors, my debts to others are many. In lively conversations I tested a number of these ideas on patient and insightful friends. A remarkable virtue of dialogue is how it frequently provides flashes of insight into quandaries puzzled over alone for long periods of time. These friends know who they are, and I thank them warmly. The readers of the manuscript, in part or in whole, added to my understanding of both the subject and my own limitations with respect to it. I thank them for each. They are M. L. Bradbury, Harry Case, Walter F. Johnson, John X. Jamrich, my brother Winston, and Praeger editor Paul Macirowski. My appreciation also to my brother Howard, who, early on, helped to fund the research required to do the project. Finally, to Helen, my wife, I owe more than a debt for long hours of typing. It is a debt that every author-spouse understands and knows can never be fully repaid.

I THE DEBT IN HUMAN PERSPECTIVE

1   Introduction

> What is government itself but the greatest of all
> reflections of human nature?
>
> — James Madison

This volume is about being human, being political, and how the two combine to influence the way members of Congress spend public money. The interplay between human nature and politics and its fiscal outcome in the power-seeking setting of Congress is the subject. The federal debt is used as an extended example, a real-world case in point. It is the vant-age point from which I view the political psychology of congressional spending.

Briefly put, the argument runs as follows: The real issue of the debt, the one underlying all other considerations, is not about what most people think. It is not about money. It is not about budgets. It is not even about debt per se. It is about people, power, and politics. The debt, at its core, is a human, not a fiscal, problem. In short, I apply to the debt James Madison's classic dictum. If, indeed, "government is the greatest of all reflections of human nature,"[1] what does that say about the debt's psychological origins and the human forces driving it?

This noneconomic approach to the debt stands in sharp contrast to our national obsession with finding a fiscal fix. Cut expenditures, conservatives argue. No, raise taxes, liberals insist. Or do both. But, I shall argue, there is no lasting fiscal fix unless there is first a human fix. Currently proposed remedies, quite typical of most reform efforts, target only symptoms and ignore the underlying cause. Rarely asked is this: What is the real cause, and will the proposed remedy correct that? In speaking of debt it is, of course, only natural to focus on revenues and expenditures. But what if the nation's unbalanced checkbook is only an end result, a symptom, and *homo politicus* the source of the problem? Should that turn out to be the case, the wisest of fiscal remedies will provide at best only temporary relief from the budget pain.

We need a larger perspective. The debt, it should be remembered, is not of recent origin. It is a worsening condition whose inception goes back over 50 years. In the period since then one can count on the fingers of one hand the years in which the federal budget was in balance. And for the past 25 years each deficit has been worse than the last.

Given this dreary fiscal history, it is folly to assume that the debt will be fixed in any permanent way by simply spending less, taxing more, or both. A more fitting response would be to assume that the debt is being propelled by a human force of uncommon power. That singular force, I intend to show, is political desire.

WHAT THIS BOOK IS *NOT* ABOUT

Another way to define what follows is by exclusion, to indicate what I do not intend to argue. I hope these exclusions will also serve to let the reader know "where I'm coming from" on this politically charged subject of the debt.

To begin, while I hope that my concern for the debt is evident on every page, my intent is not to rail against it. There has been quite enough of that. My sole purpose, rather, is to examine its political psychology and the implications that seem to flow from that.

Nor shall I wring my hands about huge federal spending, blamed so often for the debt. That old and ongoing debate between advocates of a "minimal" and "maximal" state, I believe, has been largely decided, and in favor of the latter. What is *not* decided is how to pay for it without getting eaten up by interest charges and related ills that beset nations that borrow too heavily against future earnings. The light that political psychology can shed on how and why we got into this predicament, and how we might get out, is my main concern.

I shall not argue that all deficits are bad. At war, the nation must borrow to win. Severe depressions may call for government spending beyond tax revenues. The nation's crumbling infrastructure may call for massive investments of borrowed dollars. Natural disasters may require the same.

Regrettably, most of the debt does not represent investments of this kind. A household analogy illustrates its true character. The family that borrows to fix up an old house or buy a new one usually builds future equity. But the family that borrows to pay the ordinary costs of running a household builds only debt. Most federal borrowing is of the latter kind, to pay for the ordinary costs of operating the public household. We have precious little to show for it.

I leave to others the assessment of partisan political blame for the debt. Political charges and countercharges notwithstanding, I regard deficit spending as endemic to the institution of Congress, not to one party or the other. The members of both have helped to make it so. For this reason my focus is on four characteristics of the members, none of which has anything to do with the side of the political aisle on which they sit: they are all human; they are all political; they want, most of them at least, to win reelection; and they are all skilled in using the resources of elective office, of which deficit spending is one, to guarantee that private end. These four descriptors, in my view, are far better explainers of the debt than any party label. They are the stuff of congressional behavior and the focus of this inquiry.

Finally, I do not intend to attribute to congressmen and congress-women any motives, good or bad, not found in the general population. Popular Congress bashing suggests that most of the country's venality sits under the Capitol dome. Not only is this view undeserved and unjust, it makes almost impossible a cooler search for the prime cause of the debt. In piously holding congressional members to behavioral standards higher than our own we preclude understanding their motivations *in terms of our own*. The debt exists not because they are unlike us, but because in their humanness they are precisely like us. That realization allows us to concentrate on the central question of this inquiry: What is it about their political natures that inclines them toward excessive debt?

SIX PROPOSITIONS

The argument just sketched has its foundation in six propositions about the nature of human behavior and its subset, political behavior. If these propositions do not ring true, the argument is lost. If, however, they are reasonably descriptive of the way we are, a new perspective on the debt begins to appear. It will come to be seen as a deeply human problem, one having its roots much more in behavioral psychology than in government finance.

The first proposition is this: *The main driving force behind all human behavior, political or otherwise, has its origins in the way we are as* Homo sapiens. Though highly evolved and justly proud of our civilized achievements, we are still of the family of man, not angels. Within our humanness will be found the key to what we do, the answer to the question: "Why?"

This view of behavior is neither romantic nor cynical. It is simply pragmatic. It takes human nature as it finds it. It does not deny the kindlier instincts of our nature or the shaping force of altruism. It only insists that the proper subject for the study of man is man, not some idealized image of himself.

The second proposition speaks to the question of how we manage our humanness. Publicly, we give it a gloss of rationality and respectability, denying, in effect, its origins. Clothing what we do in terms of some good other than our own, we make it socially acceptable. Hence this proposition: *Since private motivations are frequently not apparent, observed behavior — what people publicly say and do — is not a good indicator of the real reasons they do it.*

This proposition asserts that human behavior, including deficit spending, is in character something like an iceberg floating in arctic waters. What lies beneath the surface is of greater significance than that which shows above. That is what this book is about: the less visible motivations driving the deficit. They may be denied, but they cannot be dismissed in any study of deficit spending behavior.

The third proposition follows from the first two: *If behavior is rooted in our human natures, and its motivations frequently screened from view, the explanation for it will be found somewhere inside that remarkable universe called the self.*

There is always the temptation, of course, to seek the reasons for behavior outside the self. This is particularly true in fixing responsibility for the debt. There is a popular tendency to attribute it to phantoms, like "the impossible budget process," "intolerable pressures to spend," and "uncontrollable expenditures." But the budget process of Congress did not become impossible all by itself; the members made it so. Pressures to spend are, of course, intolerable. But pressures do not appropriate money; only lawmakers do that. And expenditures are not in themselves uncontrollable, except as those same lawmakers allow them to get that way. So if an explanation for the debt is to be found anywhere, it must be sought within the members' internalized needs and wants. If it cannot be found there, it has eluded us altogether.

What drives their needs and wants? In proposition four I assume that it is the same force that drives most human activity: self-interest. Adam Smith described it well for the economic arena, and I think his description applies to the political arena, too. Said the author of *The Wealth of Nations*: "Man has almost constant occasion for the help of his brethren, and it is in vain for him to expect it from their benevolence only. . . . It is not from the benevolence of the butcher, the brewer, or the baker, that we expect our dinner, but from their regard for their own interest."[2] It is not out of the benevolence of our representatives in Congress that we should expect our governmental fare, "but from their regard for their own self-interests."

The proposition is this: *Members of Congress are maximizers of their self-interests; they engage in activities that best advance them and shun those that damage them. The debt can be understood only within that behavioral context.*

Proposition five focuses on public money as the servant of political self-interests. No other kind of money serves those interests better, including money from Political Action Committees (PACs). The attention PAC money is getting these days leaves a false impression about the nature of its influence. To be sure, this influence is alarmingly great. But what is often forgotten is that if the members of Congress did not have power over the public purse, PACs would abandon them like the plague. PACs make campaign contributions to incumbents only in the prospect of fiscal favors returned. It follows then that the more public money the members spend, the more private money they can attract. Hence this proposition: *No other single power than that to appropriate and spend can influence the political fortunes of congressmen and congresswomen more; access to public money is where political self-interest and opportunity meet.*

Proposition six transcends all the rest, for it carries the analysis beyond both the fiscal and the psychological to the question of statecraft, how we are governed. It is this: *At its ultimate, the debt issue is about the kind of representative government we want and deserve. Deficit spending produces one kind, balanced budgets quite another.*

So sweeping a proposition demands a fulsome explanation and defense; it will be forthcoming in due course. For now, however, this needs to be said: The more one thinks about borrowing and taxing as political behavior, not just two ways to finance the costs of government, the more one realizes that he is dealing with two very different forms of governance, the one on the shoddy side, the other more in keeping with an open democracy. Borrowing, an "in-house" affair with Congress, is done simply by voting to raise the debt ceiling, so common now it is almost ritual. Taxing, by contrast, inevitably raises a raucous public debate, an absolute essential for a vigorous democracy. It is glasnost applied to the fiscal affairs of government, but borrowing is its secretive opposite.

The great political irony is this: In the very act of thwarting public discussion and debate, borrowing facilitates political ambition. Taxing, by contrast, in making congressmen and congresswomen defend their spending against all comers chastens and sobers political ambition. So, while borrowing serves private political purposes well, it serves democratic statecraft ill. But taxing works just the opposite. It serves political purposes ill but democracy well. If these essays do nothing else, I hope they will take a small step toward redefining what the debt debate should really be about. It should be much less about money and much more about how we are governed. Members of Congress will, of course, keep the focus on money; citizens, however, should, as much as they dislike taxes, insist on that form of finance, because in the end it produces better government and, I believe, at the least cost.

SOME PONDERABLES

Turn now from the argument and its underlying propositions to some of the problems confronted in pursuing an inquiry like this. I refer especially to the terms of reference and choice of source material. With respect to terms of reference, consider the concept of human nature. A slipper quarry, it is without a universally agreed upon meaning. Webster's Third New International Edition doesn't even try for one. Instead, it devotes a column inch of fine print to a variety of definitions, acknowledging along the way the conflict between those who claim that human nature is socially acquired and those who insist it is inborn. For my purpose here I shall regard human nature simply as reflecting those behaviors, attitudes, and ideas that people acquire somehow. We have them; that is what counts. Further, we have this assortment of behaviors, attitudes, and ideas in common, enough at least so that socially we can be defined as human.

Then there is the matter of defining political nature. Is it a special kind of nature, or is it simply human nature expressing itself in political settings? As stated earlier, I opt for the latter, believing that men and women in politics are not a breed apart. They are simply human beings whose natures are shaped by the demands of politics, in the same way that businesspeople are shaped by the demands of enterprise.

Here I am especially interested in the nature of professional politicians, those who make their livings at politics. The reason is obvious: Congress long ago ceased to be a "citizens' legislature" as the Founding Fathers had envision it. It is now composed almost entirely of career politicians dependent upon holding onto their seats for both their livelihoods and psychological satisfactions. Since it would be hard to overestimate the impact of these two factors on their spending, I shall have to examine with some care the connections between a deep personal investment in a congressional seat and fiscal behavior.

As for source materials, what hunting ground does one stake out for the study of Congress, human nature, and the federal debt? Recent advances in the social sciences make that a difficult question to resolve. When I first began the present inquiry a few years back, I assumed, too hastily it turned out, that I was picking up again on political psychology, a matter explored years earlier in my doctoral dissertation. And I still think of this effort that way, but with a much enlarged view of political psychology. Today many of the social sciences have something to contribute to political psychology, for most have been won over to the "behavioral persuasion," the study of real human beings rather than abstractions. As a result, the number and variety of disciplinary resources available have literally exploded. Hard choices about where to invest time and effort have had to be made. The following are just a few of the academic vineyards, outside traditional political psychology, where I have found the harvest good.[3]

Economics was the earliest of the social sciences to define the human variable in its investigations. Economic man, human nature under market conditions, has, since the time of Adam Smith, been carefully documented and described. At first glance economic man, bent on making a profit, would appear to be no kin to political man, whose concern is with governance. But in fact, some of the most evocative current contributions to an understanding of political behavior are coming from political economists pointing out the striking parallels between the two. Both political and economic man are entrepreneurs; both seek gain. The drives propelling their respective efforts spring from a single source: the human nature they share in common. No inquiry into the human side of the debt can ignore these rich contributions from political economists.

While political science was much slower than economics to place flesh and blood people at the center of its formulations (the earlier emphasis was on institutions), the focus now is unmistakable. It is on political behavior. Once this shift began to occur, in the first quarter of this century, political science became a rich resource for the study of *homo politicus*.

Certain areas of sociological thought offer useful concepts for understanding the interconnections among Congress, human nature, and the federal debt. I refer particularly to the work on the nature of power and influence in social, economic, and political systems. Congress's excessive spending without taxing represents an enormous shift of power to itself and away from citizens. We need to understand the anatomy of this shift and its critical meaning for both citizens and their representatives.

Beyond the social sciences there are the humanistic studies, such as philosophy, both moral and political. Political philosophers from the time of the ancient Greeks made certain assumptions about human nature and upon these erected their conceptions of what government ought to do and be. From Plato and Aristotle on there has always been the implicit assumption that human nature and politics were so intertwined that one cannot speak of one without the other.

Moral philosophy is a subject I was determined to stay away from in this study. Leave the moralizing about the debt to others, I told myself. I have changed my mind. The more I dug into the matter, the more I realized that the act of spending without taxing has immense moral and ethical implications. Those cannot be denied and must be wrestled with. Moral philosophers' concern with man's relation to the state, and vice versa, is right on target.

Other gleanings will become apparent from references as matters unfold. The reader will have already observed, however, that my approach is eclectic. Like a hunter in the field, I have gone where my sense of the situation led, based on my own study and experience as a perennial observer of congressional behavior.

One other thing must also now be apparent. No single source speaks directly to my subject: the interconnections of Congress, human nature, and the federal debt. Multitudes of sources speak to one or another of the three, but there is no body of literature, research, or experience that speaks to their organic unity. As a result, I have had to think that matter through quite on my own, and not without a frequent sense of despair and loneliness. Only the reader can judge the results.

WHY MEMBERS OF CONGRESS?

In closing this introduction I should like to make explicit that which I trust has been implicit, namely, my reason for focusing on congressmen and congresswomen when, in fact, many others besides them are also responsible for the debt. The president, for example, prepares the budget and recommends levels of spending; a good case could be made regarding his involvement. But as Senator Garn once reminded his colleagues, "The fact of the matter is no President of the United States has ever spent a dime not appropriated by Congress. A President can recommend a budget, he can yell, scream, plead, shout, veto, but ultimately, he does not spend any money not appropriated by Congress. . . . Every single dime of the $2 trillion deficit and above has been appropriated by the Congress of the United States — no one else."

Bureaucrats are not free of blame. Their ranks, perks, and salaries are tied to the size of their departmental budgets, and they constantly lobby for more money. Beyond officialdom, there is the army of lobbyists, all pressuring for fiscal favors. And how about the rest of us, who are not above badgering our congressmen for government handouts, all the while stubbornly refusing to pay more taxes? "Lay off Congress," it could well be argued; "it is only giving constituents what they want."

That protest has merit, *unless one is inquiring into psychological first causes*. In that case, one must abandon the easy assumption that since many are implicated, all are equally responsible. One must seek out, instead, those persons who are most psychologically predisposed to borrow and empowered to borrow. Put that way, prime responsibility for the debt becomes very clear: Of the entire cast in this melancholy drama, congressmen and congresswomen are unmistakably the leading actors. They have the greatest desire to engage in deficit spending, the greatest opportunity, and the fewest possible political risks. Not to spend to excess would be almost unhuman. From the viewpoint of behavior, then, any group in this constant state of psychological readiness must be brought into the very center of the search for first causes. In short, the argument is that Congress long ago ignited the "big bang" in deficit spending and continues to fuel it to this day.

In closing, a note about the reason for the essay that follows. It came rather late in my writing; at first I had not planned on it at all. I simply assumed there was no need to trace out historically the intimate connection between politics and human nature. But upon further reflection, I decided that would be like trying to erect a building without first laying a foundation. It was not only out of his personal experience that James Madison asserted that government is "the greatest of all reflections of human nature." It was also out of his long sense of history, and understanding of political philosophy, that he said it. I trust that the brief historical sketch that follows will provide a sufficient foundation for the claim of this volume that the debt, too, is one of the greatest of all reflections of human nature.

2 Politics and Human Nature: Voices from the Past

> To talk of politics without reference to human beings ... is just the deepest error in our political thinking.
> — Walter Lippmann

Ideas, in the course of their development, rarely follow a predictable path; false starts and failures often mark their course. Intellectual history is much like a freight train that constantly shunts old cars to weed-strewn sidings, while sending shiny new ones hurtling on their way to uncertain fates.

But some ideas are different: They persist and even gather force with the passing years. Why?

One can only speculate, but three qualities seem to inhere in those ideas that outlast others. First, they arise in human experience. They are not fabrications of the mind; they are instead of the fabric of life. Thoughtful persons, when considering them, are apt to say, "Yes, I have found that to be true." Second, while mirroring human experience, lasting ideas are not dogmatic about it; they allow for change. They recognize the pliant quality of human experience, its magnificent capacity for adaptation. This is another way of saying that their truth is large, rather than parochial. Finally, and always, ideas that stand up to time have utility in that they explain human experience. They help to make sense of it.

The idea that human nature is a determining force in politics, a notion that is as old as any in Western political thought, has these three characteristics. It arose out of the experience of the ancient Greeks, those shrewd observers of political men. For them it became axiomatic that where politics is there also is human nature, demanding its due. This idea's pliant quality was demonstrated when it went underground during the long Dark Ages, only to burst forth again during the Renaissance, this time transformed to fit a new age. And its utility for moderns was reaffirmed by Walter Lippmann when he reminded in his *Preface to Politics* that to consider politics without taking human nature into account "is just the deepest error in our political thinking."[1]

Yet there is among us democratic moderns an ambivalence about this idea. In spite of its long history and contemporary affirmation, our understanding of its true meaning is largely intellectual. We have difficulty grasping, at some deeper level of meaning, the reality that human nature is the catalyst of politics and that as catalyst it alters outcomes. That difficulty is clearly apparent in popular views of the debt. Seldom considered is the role of human nature in it. The possibility that human nature might be its catalyst does not get seriously examined.

And the reason may be that such an examination requires a certain pragmatic view of human nature, one that enables the viewer to turn off the public noise of politics and listen, instead, to the messages of the political heart. To assist in that is the purpose of this essay. Political thinkers from the earliest times have been very clear about the relationship of human nature to politics. It constituted for them the point of beginning and, I might add, a skeptical point of beginning. Upon it they then constructed their schemes of government. Human nature was the given, politics the variable. We need that kind of approach to the debt problem now. To solve it we must confront the human factor first. If we can do that, a fiscal solution may follow quite naturally.

For convenience, I have let chronology organize the brief historical perspective that follows. Representative thinkers among the ancients are presented first, then those of the Renaissance and immediately following, and finally the moderns.

THE ANCIENTS

Like many seminal ideas in Western thought, the linkage between politics and human nature began with Plato and Aristotle. For Plato, man's physiology determined his human nature and, by extension, his politics.[2] Plato came at the connection in this fashion: Using the physiology and psychology of his day, he correlated aspects of human nature with parts of the body, for example, intelligence with the head, courage with the heart, and moderation with the abdomen. The just government, he concluded, was one in which these salutary qualities found in human nature work in harmonious cooperation. Good government was, in effect, good human nature applied to the affairs of state.

While Plato's psychology was crude and quickly abandoned, his method for coming at the relationship between human nature and politics set a pattern for all political thinkers who were to follow: In matters political start with human nature, not government. A good government is one that is based upon a wise conception of the way we are as human beings.

Aristotle, more the scientist than philosopher Plato, believed that knowledge was best derived by direct observation. So, in *The Politics,* a classic on government to this day, he observed and analyzed *homo politicus* and the institution called the state.[3]

As for human nature and politics, Aristotle was more explicit than Plato, and he carried the implications much further. While Plato reasoned in steps from physiology, to human nature, to politics, Aristotle connected them organically. We are *born* political animals, his observations told him. He cited as evidence the fact that people, left to their own devices, inevitably engage in politics. Further, gather enough of them together and they will form common protective associations, another name for states.

And what about human nature in governance? Aristotle appears to have been more than cautious: He was skeptical. Otherwise he would not have gone outside the state for his model for managing it. What he did was cast about for a social institution in which human nature operated in the best interest of all its members. He found it in the well-ordered human family. Such a family possessed two qualities that Aristotle thought essential for the state. These two, at first glance, may seem incompatible, an odd coupling, but Aristotle had apparently observed that one could not exist without the other. On the one hand, the well-ordered family showed equal care and concern for all its members, whether young or old, healthy or ill, able to work or not. On the other, it recognized the importance of limits; it lived within its means. For Aristotle, the ability to live within limits was as important for the public household as it was for the private. Upon it depended the ability to exercise genuine care and concern. Only the solvent state could be a genuine welfare state.

RENAISSANCE AND BEYOND

It would be nearly 17 centuries before another political thinker would revive and carry on the Aristotelian tradition of direct observation of human nature in politics. And he did it with such unrelenting scrutiny that his name has become synonymous with political skulduggery. He was, of course, Niccolò Machiavelli (1469–1527), the Italian author of *The Prince*.[4]

Machiavelli

While Machiavelli's mind may not have ranged as widely as Aristotle's, he far outdid the Greek in minute political analysis. In examining the human nature of his tyrant prince, to whom he was an adviser, Machiavelli expounded on the qualities of cruelty, infidelity, and hypocrisy, showing the advantages and disadvantages of each in governing. Though most of Machiavelli's political works had been published earlier by papal authority, they were reconsidered by Rome in 1559 and placed on the first Index of Forbidden Books. But Machiavelli had long before made his point, writ large: Political thinking devoid of allowances for even the worst in human nature is no thinking at all.

Machiavelli's unsavory reputation notwithstanding, *The Prince* reveals as astute an analysis of human nature and politics as ever written. An example is the distinction he made between the state and those who would rule over it. The rulers are human beings, he observed, who are subject to all the frailties that flesh is heir to. But the state is an institution, the creation of covenants and constitutions. The two should never be confused as being the same.

At first blush, Machiavelli's distinction seems obvious and unnecessary to make, until one begins to think of the human meaning of partisan political struggle. Then one begins to appreciate Machiavelli's worldly sense of political psychology. Partisan political struggle, he concluded, is an entirely autonomous human affair, completely apart from the state. The whole purpose of partisan fights is predatory, to capture the state in order to gain and maintain political power. And how about the state's social purposes? They too are but means to the same end. The end is power, first, last, always. The means are anything that advances it. The state is the supreme prize. All political efforts must be judged against their ability to capture and hold it.

While many subsequent political thinkers would criticize Machiavelli for concentrating on man's darker side, it must be said in his favor that he advanced the claims of realism in the analysis of political behavior.

Following Machiavelli, the Aristotelian tradition of direct observation of political behavior went into sharp decline, replaced by philosophers who preferred to speculate about human nature as it was in its natural state. Their assumption was that to know what kind of government was best it was essential to know what human nature was like before the trappings of civilization contaminated it. The object of government, then, became that of helping to restore man to his original state. Three men, Thomas Hobbes (1588–1679), John Locke (1634–1704), and Jean-Jacques Rousseau (1712–1778), were of the natural state school of political thought.

Thomas Hobbes

Hobbes's view of human nature as he described it in *The Leviathan* was dark and dour.[5] And his remedy for that condition was the same. Men may be born free, equal, and with natural rights, he acknowledged, but they are also born brutes. Left to their own devices, they are constantly at one another's throats. "A war of all against all" Hobbes called the natural human condition.

Why are men like that? Hobbes's answer is curious: It is because they are equal. Equality fuels competition for scarce resources, inspires mutual distrust, and fires the love of glory. It makes one man invade for gain, another for safety, yet another for reputation.

And what is the social effect of this war of all against all? It produces a deprived state in which there is no industry, trade, or agriculture and "no knowledge of the face of the earth; no account of time; no arts; no letters; no society; and worst of all continual fear, and the danger of violent death. . . ."

Upon this dour prospect of human nature Hobbes erected his political remedy: absolute dictatorship. The only way that men, who were both brutish and equal, could avoid self-annihilation was to surrender to an absolute sovereign all of their natural rights and prerogatives. Further, they must regard the sovereign himself as incapable of doing wrong, no matter how severe and oppressive his actions may be. The result, Hobbes asserted, was still preferable to a war of all against all.

What shall we say today of Hobbes's view of human nature and politics? Few democratic moderns would take kindly to it. But there was in Hobbes, as there was in Machiavelli, a needed political realism, a recognition that man's darker side exists, that it can easily insinuate itself into the body politic and, if not controlled, is capable of producing evil.

John Locke

Locke had no truck with dictatorship, but with Hobbes he believed that men were born free and equal. The problem arose when they entered into compacts with governments to protect those rights. Just as pristine human nature could be corrupted without government, it could also be corrupted by government, Locke maintained. Indeed, governments, being more powerful than enemies in the natural state, could be more cruel. Locke saw the difference as that between polecats and foxes on the one hand, and lions on the other. "It is inconceivable," he wrote in *Two Treatises,* "that people would be so foolish that they care to avoid what mischiefs may be done by polecats and foxes, but are content, nay think it safe, to be devoured by lions."[6]

Locke's answer to the human problem in politics, then, was to assume the potential for trouble and to hedge against it in compacts with government. It was an idea that Jean-Jacques Rousseau also found attractive.

Jean-Jacques Rousseau

"I will venture to say," Rousseau wrote in his *Confessions,* "that I am like no one in the whole world. I may be no better, but, at least, I am different." And indeed, the French philosopher was different. Primitive man was not rapacious and cruel like Hobbes maintained, he protested, constantly engaged in a war of all against all. "Nothing is more gentle than man in his primitive state," he wrote, "as he is placed by nature an equal distance from the stupidity of brutes."[7]

Then why are men capable of being brutish? Rousseau's answer was that they are diseased by false culture, enslaved by baubles, as it were, causing them to lose their sense of their own natural and authentic worth. Discovering how to reclaim that worth was the task that Rousseau put his mind to in much of his writing.

As for politics, Rousseau took man, as he found him in his natural state, to be virtuous and then set out to create a civil order, "a sure and legitimate rule of administration," as he put it. What was required to free man from his chains was a stable political system that combined both freedom and security. "The problem," he wrote, "is to find a form of association which will defend and protect with the whole common force the persons and goods of each associate, and in which each, while uniting himself with all, may still obey himself alone, and remain free as before."

With Locke, Rousseau believed in a social contract with the governors. But Rousseau's contract sounded much like Hobbes's solution to the war of all against all, for every person had to hand over to the rulers all his powers and rights. Rousseau argued, however, that the social contract actually provided more freedom because citizens themselves made and shaped the rulers. The rulers thus became what he called a "General Will," the embodiment of everybody's wishes and wants. And this "General Will" could be relied upon to look after the "preservation and welfare of every part."

For Rousseau, the creation of a General Will was the splendid part of the social contract. It would always decree true liberty for all. The result? "An inalienable, indivisible, and infallible sovereign whose commands are really liberating laws. . . . Thus, what man loses by the social contract is his natural liberty . . . he gains in civil liberty."

In contrast to Aristotle and Machiavelli, these three natural state philosophers were long on speculations about human nature and short on analysis of actual political behavior. As a result there was in their schemes a distinct blind spot: They ignored the motivations of rulers themselves. Hobbes did not even care what motives drove his absolute dictator. Nor was he concerned about the dictator's methods, so long as he kept brutish men from one another's throats. John Locke recognized rulers' capacity for evil and for that reason sought to limit their powers. But one will not find in Locke any explanation of why they act like lions rather than mere polecats and foxes. And Rousseau's blind faith in his social contract kept him from dealing realistically with the possibility that the rulers might find it in their self-interests to subvert it.

Jeremy Bentham

This tendency of natural state philosophers to ignore the motivations of rulers was also evident in Jeremy Bentham (1748–1832), the British jurist and master of turgid, convoluted prose. (A contemporary of Bentham's once observed that it would have been nice had he been translated into English!) Bentham saw himself as a counselor to legislators, advising them in his brand of human psychology, the better to control their constituents. Since he regarded his psychology as universal, the reader can only assume that legislators were also governed by it, but Bentham never got around to saying that. Nor did he ever hint how his psychology might actually operate within the ruling class.

That, however, is where any similarity between Bentham and the natural state philosophers ends, for he began an entirely new mode of inquiry into human nature. Abandoning the earlier attempt to interpret politics in terms of an assumed original state, Bentham began to analyze conduct in terms of motives. And in this attempt he must be regarded as a precursor of modern-day behavioral psychology. He set his prodigious mind to work on this question: What single motivation, above all others, exerts the greatest influence on human behavior? To qualify, that motive would have to exhibit certain desirable characteristics: All men should be propelled by it; it should help predict behavior; and most of all, it should suggest what kind of government is best.

A tall order, but Bentham found that all-controlling motivation in the concept of happiness. As Bentham concluded in his *Principles of Morals and Legislation,* happiness is the single most powerful force driving human behavior.[8]

Having arrived at that conclusion, Bentham then inquired into the subproperties of happiness. He found them in pleasure and its opposite, pain. "Nature has placed mankind under the governance of two souvereign masters, *pain and pleasure,*" he wrote. "It is for them to point out what we ought to do, as well as to determine what we shall do. They govern us in all we do, in all we say, in all we think."

Bentham cataloged human pains and pleasures. Included in the latter are the pleasures of the senses, wealth, skill, amity, good name, and power. The pleasures of senses included taste, smell, touch, hearing, seeing, sex, and health. The pleasures of wealth are those of gain, acquisition, and possession. Skill is a pleasure because of the enjoyment of putting particular instruments to their uses. The pleasures of amity are those of being on good terms with good friends. A good name affords pleasure because it brings love and esteem. The pleasures of power are those "that accompany the persuasion of a man's being in a condition to dispose people, by means of their hopes and fears, to give him the benefit of their services."

Bentham's catalog of pains included those of privation, disappointment, and the senses. The pains of privation are those of "unsatisfied desire." Those of disappointment take place when "enjoyment happens to have been looked for, . . . and that expectation is made suddenly to cease. . . . Pains of the senses include hunger, thirst, bad taste, disagreeable sights and sounds, excessive heat and cold, disease, overexertion, enmity and an ill name."

Motives, for Bentham, were "substantially nothing more than pleasure or pain, operating in a certain manner." They are to be "understood as anything whatsoever, which, by influencing the will of a sensitive being, is supposed to serve as a means of determining him to act, or voluntarily to forbear to act, upon an occasion."

Having located the wellsprings of human behavior in the concept of happiness and cataloged the various sorts of pains and pleasures and their corresponding motives, Bentham was ready to conclude what kind of government was right and proper. It was that government that provided the greatest happiness for the greatest number. And that formulation defined the task of a legislator. "Pleasures, then, and the avoidance of pains, are the ends which the legislator has in view," he wrote. "It behooves him therefore to understand their value. Pleasures and pains are the instruments he has to work with: It behooves him therefore to understand their force."

How shall we evaluate Bentham's approach to human nature in politics? Ralph Waldo Emerson called it a "stinking philosophy." And John Maynard Keynes agreed. "It is a worm that has been gnawing at the insides of modern civilization and is responsible for the present moral decay," the British economist declared. But political scientist Harold Laski, also British, took a kindlier view. "If Bentham had possessed [David] Hume's exquisite style instead of his own barbarous convolutions," he asserted, "political science would have been fifty years ahead of its present position."

His critics and supporters aside, this much must be said for Bentham: After him it would be hard not to construe the behavior of legislators as a response to the motives embedded in human nature. But since he thought only in terms of their use by legislators on constituents, we are left to speculate on how he thought those same motives influenced their own political behavior.

MODERN

Many political thinkers in this century contributed substantially to an understanding of the role of human nature in politics. Two, however, stand out. Graham Wallas and Walter Lippmann each made distinctively separate contributions, but they were together on one fundamental about human nature and its implication for politics: Self-interest was the central driving force in human nature, and as a result, politics is essentially a nonrational enterprise, more informed by the heart than the head.

Graham Wallas

If one were to pick a date inaugurating the study of modern political psychology, it would be 1908, the year Wallas published the first edition of his *Human Nature in Politics*.[9] Reprinted in 1910, 1920, and 1948 and again in 1962, the book has continued to have a shaping influence on that subject even to this day. And the reason is not hard to find. Wallas combined a deep philosophic knowledge of political theory with a practitioner's keen sense of its human nuances. An Oxford University don in political philosophy, Wallas was also a longtime activist in the hurly-burly of City of London elective politics. *Human Nature in Politics* for this reason has both the earthiness of a political practitioner and the deep understanding of a long-time scholar and teacher of the subject.

Wallas made much of what he called the "rationalist fallacy" in politics. Men are not guided by "enlightened self interest," he observed. Their *own* self-interest, rather, is what determines their behavior. He believed this was not only true of politicians but was characteristic of human behavior generally. A man's action, he wrote, is not the result of an "intellectual process of some end which he desires and then calculates the means by which that end can be obtained." To the contrary, "impulses such as personal affection, fear, ridicule, the desire for property, etc., are better guides to why men behave as they do." It was from this realistic view of human nature that Wallas derived his definition of politics. It "consists largely," he maintained, "in the exploitation of subconscious, non-rational inference." In other words, politics is the art of manipulating the feelings of the heart rather than appealing to the logic of the mind. In this view one can hear strong echoes of Jeremy Bentham.

Graham Wallas, however, was neither resigned to nor accepting of this observed domination of politics by human nature. "All right," he seemed to be saying, "so men don't act out of enlightened self-interest. So they do follow their own self-centered desires. But does that relieve us of trying to find ways to create a good society?" He did not think so, and his active involvement in politics was testimony to that belief. We must do more than recognize the realities of human nature as we find them, he asserted. We must also probe for new perspectives on the operation of human nature in an effort to both interpret it better and better predict its workings.

Wallas's conviction that politics was not a lost cause was based on his reading of history. "The whole progress of human civilization beyond its earliest stages," he wrote, "has been made possible by the invention of methods of thought which enable us to *interpret* and *forecast* the working of nature more successfully than we could if we merely followed the line of least resistance in the use of our minds."[10] Wallas's plea was for "a new vision of human nature and human possibilities," permitting people to take "a conscious part in the great adventure of discovering ways of living open to all, which all can believe to be good."

Walter Lippmann

Graham Wallas's realistic, yet saving, view of human nature in politics was not lost on his onetime student Walter Lippmann. For over three decades a perceptive commentator on the American political scene, Lippmann agreed with his mentor that people, not institutions, were the key to understanding political activity. His comments on Wallas's times and work are instructive on this point. "In the midst of a bustle of activity," Lippmann wrote of the turn-of-the-century period, "politics appeared to have no center to which its thinking could be referred. The truth was driven home upon him [Wallas] that political science is a science of human relationships with humans left out. So he writes that nearly all of the students of politics analyze institutions and avoid the analysis of man."[11]

Lippmann reinforced Wallas's assessment of early political science. "Graham Wallas," he said, "touched the cause of the trouble when he pointed out that political science today discusses institutions and ignores the nature of men who make and live under them, and anyone who has absorbed his insight has an intellectual ground work for political observation. When we recognize that the focus of politics is shifting from a mechanical to a human center we shall have reached what is, I believe, the most essential idea of modern politics."[12]

Walter Lippmann, however, was quick to perceive limitations in Wallas's work, especially defined as political psychology. "He has not produced a political psychology," Lippmann wrote, "but has written a manifesto for it."[13] But if Lippmann was skeptical about the finality of Wallas's work as political psychology, he was not about his basic proposition regarding the nonrational character of human behavior. "The attempts of theorists," he wrote, "to explain man's success as rational acts and his failures as lapses of reason have always ended in a dismal and misty unreality." And that applied to the practice of politics, too. "No genuine politician ever treats his constituents as reasoning animals," Lippmann went on. "Only the pathetic amateur deludes himself into thinking that if he presents the major and minor premise, the voter will automatically draw the conclusion on election day. The successful politician — good or bad — deals with dynamics, with the will, the hopes, the needs and visions of men."[14]

Lippmann also concurred with Wallas that accepting the centrality of human nature was not enough. "To accept that nature does not mean that we accept its present character. It is probably true that the impulses of men have changed very little within recorded history. What has changed enormously from epoch to epoch is the character in which these impulses appear. The impulses that at one period work themselves out into cruelty and lust may at another produce the richest values in the world. The statesman can effect that choice. His business is to provide fine opportunities to surround childhood, youth and age with homes, schools, cities and countryside that shall be stocked with interest and the chance for generous activity."[15]

SUMMARY

From Plato to Lippmann the evidence seems clear: Politics mirrors human nature. It is impossible to speak of one without the other. Views of human nature may alter through time, as may notions of what type of government best becomes it. But the intimacy of the relationship has never been seriously questioned. Nor has the implied conclusion: To study political behavior begin not with its outward forms; start, instead, with human nature.

Now, if one were to take that advice and apply it to the fiscal affairs of government, to what conclusions might he be drawn? How three of the world's foremost thinkers on economics and politics answered that question, and one exactly contrary to the other two, is the subject of the next essay.

3 Household Finances: Private and Public

> Seeing then, that the state is made up of households, before speaking of the state we must speak of the management of households.
>
> — Aristotle

Great men embody the great issues of their times. In their persons the issues are joined, the whole story is told. Who, for example, can think of the American Revolution without the image of Washington appearing before him? Or that of Lincoln in the case of slavery? Winston Churchill's bulldog countenance will forever symbolize Britain's determination to survive the onslaught of Hitler.

One of the great issues in the deficit debate is embodied in the lives of three men: Aristotle, Adam Smith, and John Maynard Keynes. Though divided by centuries, their thoughts on the proper financing of government embody much of the story. I therefore call them to my aid in this essay.

The issue is this: Should the state, or the public household, be required to live within the same fiscal restraints as the private household?[1] Families, for example, must, within reason, live within their means. Should the state also? At home, new expenditures must be matched, sooner or later, by new income. Should the state be required to attach new tax bills to each new spending measure? If a family borrows, it must pay back, and on schedule. Should the state be required to do likewise?

Aristotle launched the debate on those questions in *The Politics*.[2] Smith elaborated and reinforced Aristotle's position in *The Wealth of Nations*,[3] and Keynes mounted formidable arguments against it in his *General Theory*.[4]

ARISTOTLE

When one visits Athens he can seek out a certain ancient sun-dappled olive grove not far from the Acropolis and imagine that he is standing on hallowed ground. And he is if, as legend has it, this was the site of Plato's Academy. For here the illustrious philosopher and master teacher, gathering about him the bright young men of his time, launched a series of powerful ideas that changed forever the way we think about our Western world.

One of the students who came to learn from Plato was a youth of eighteen, attracted to Athens in the first place, it is presumed, by the same magnetism that has always drawn bright young men to shining cities. His name was Aristotle and he stayed with Plato for over twenty years, building his intellectual capital.

As a young man, Aristotle was not a particularly pleasant fellow. Indeed, he was considered something of a dandy and spoke with a lisp. It was an affectation, some scholars have speculated, aimed at compensating for his middle-class background. At any rate, he stood in sharp contrast to his elite and erudite master, who thought that only philosophers were fit to be kings. But Plato liked Aristotle, for he found in him a craggy mind and dry, relentless wit. As a student he stood out above all the rest, and today his name is remembered alongside that of his illustrious master.

While he was with Plato, Aristotle started work on a book on the science of government; he would finish it years later, after he had matured his thoughts on the subject. Titled simply *The Politics,* it would launch a series of powerful ideas that would change forever how we think about government. When the reader scans the contents of *The Politics,* he may find it to be a curious, even puzzling experience. Here is one of the great classics on government, and yet almost the entire first part is devoted, of all things, to household management. Baffled, one asks, "Why?" Could it be that Aristotle made a mistake? Or did the editor inadvertently slip into the manuscript a section from another of Aristotle's numerous works?

The opening pages, however, quickly dispel those initial suspicions. Aristotle knew exactly what he was up to. When speaking of the public household, he found that the private household provided the best perspective from which to view it. It, he decided, should be the model for the fiscal management of the state.

Why?

Aristotle drew his reasons from his knowledge of both the natural and social sciences. As a natural scientist, Aristotle gave priority to the private household because it was an integral part of the public household (like a stem's relationship to a leaf) and because one is dependent on the other. "We must look at the least elements of which the state is composed," he said. "Whether a state or anything else, this is the way to obtain the clearest view of them."

So it was the logic of natural science that caused Aristotle to assert, as in the quotation at the beginning of this essay: "Seeing then, that the state is made up of households before speaking of the state we must speak of the management of households."[5] It was in the natural order of things.

As a social scientist searching for ruling principles, Aristotle asked two prior questions before putting the fiscal one: "What form of household management best helps the family to reach its goals?" and "What form of political community is best of all for those who are most able to realize their ideal life?" Then comes the economic question: "What fiscal principles should govern both the houses?"

Aristotle found those principles in household management, and he commended them to the state. In fact, one gets the impression that Aristotle could not even conceive of a state that would not be governed by these same principles. That he found it unthinkable was evidenced by the fact that he never proposed any economic rules for the state other than those that he found in a well-ordered private household.

What were these principles?

Paramount among them was the principle of "limits" or "scarcity." Every household, he found, is constrained by economic limits and scarcities. The rule applies to all households, regardless of their affluence or lack of it. Even prosperous households experience limits and scarcities, for while wealth may be expandable, it is not indefinitely so. There are always finite limits. Inevitably there comes a time when one must manage within the limits of his means or court disaster. Said Aristotle: "The amount of property which is needed for a good life is not unlimited . . . there is a boundary fixed."

What if "wants" exceed the "boundary fixed"? Human nature being what it is, Aristotle expected that they would, but seemed impatient with those who cannot scale their wants down to conform to limits and scarcities. He called wants "insatiable" and therefore "unnatural." They must be constrained.

In the realities of limits and scarcities Aristotle saw two implications for household management. First, the common good is best served
by "internal controls" that balance expenditures against available
resources. Second, sharing within the household should be aimed at
satisfying "basic needs," like food, shelter, and clothing, rather than
every want.

So also in the state. "Some limit must be imposed [for] the avarice of
mankind is insatiable. . . . Men always want more and more without
end. . . . It is in the nature of desire not to be satisfied and most men
live only for the gratifications of it. . . . The greatest crimes are caused
by excess and not necessity."

All this may make Aristotle sound like a crusty old fiscal
conservative, insensitive to human needs and aspirations. But that
would be a hasty judgment on the Greek, for he found within the family certain liberal human values that he thought worthy of emulation
by the state. He simply seemed to feel that liberal action had its best
chance when due attention was paid to limits and scarcities. Conservative economic management, he seemed to be saying, was, in the long
run, the best way to assure the resources needed to support liberal
politics.

Among the household values that Aristotle liked, he emphasized two.
First, he liked the household's sense of justice, for it is based on human,
rather than property, values. "The business of household management,"
he wrote, "is more concerned with the good condition of human beings
than it is with the good condition of property."

And Aristotle liked the domestic household's method of distributing
its limited resources among its members. It rests in the recognition that
some contribute more than others — for example, parents and other
adults more than children and the able-bodied more than the infirm — yet
all share equally in terms of basic necessities.

But as we said, the satisfaction of these values depended upon living
within limits and scarcity. If wants, which are insatiable and unnatural,
were permitted to run wild, the provisions of even the basic necessities
may be threatened. For that reason, "some limit must be imposed . . .
there is a boundary fixed."

What was Aristotle's contribution to the debate? Ironically, it was to
direct attention away from the state to one of its "least parts," the well-
ordered household. That was the way, he argued, to obtain the "clearest
view" of how the state should be managed. It was an idea of enduring
value and power, but it would be almost 2,000 years before Adam Smith
would bring it to full flower.

ADAM SMITH

Adam Smith's plain gravestone in the churchyard in Cannongate, Scotland, bears the date July 17, 1790, and, underneath, this simple inscription: "Author, *The Wealth of Nations.*"

For ordinary mortals a single title would seem to be a modest obituary, giving at best a limited claim to fame. But for Adam Smith *The Wealth of Nations* was quite enough. Two hundred years after his death, he is still regarded as a towering figure in economic thought and *The Wealth of Nations,* which is still widely read in most of the major languages of the world, as an authentic classic.

The Wealth of Nations is more than a book. It is, rather, an outpouring of life, rich in its breadth of knowledge, illuminating in its cutting generalizations, and bold in its vision. Almost impossible to summarize, it is like a great feast of many delectable courses, each of which deserves to be savored.

Still, if one were forced to select a single sentence from this vast work that seems best to express Adam Smith's attitude toward fiscal affairs in the state, it would be one drawn almost directly, it would appear, from Aristotle. For, like the Greek, Smith drew an analogy between the family household and the state. Said he: "What is prudent in every private family can scarce be folly in that of a great kingdom." Frugality, not profligacy, was for Adam Smith the cardinal virtue, and public budgets should be in balance, just as they are required to be in a well-ordered domestic household.

The force of Adam Smith's ideas is best experienced in his own rich imagery and cadenced prose.

On the profligacy of rulers: "They are themselves always, and without exception, the greatest spendthrifts of society." [Since that is the case,] "it is the highest impertinence and presumption in kings and ministers to pretend to watch over the economy of private people. . . . Let them look well after their own expense, and they may safely trust private people with theirs. If their own extravagance does not ruin the state, that of their subjects never will."[6]

On the consequences of government spending: "Almost the whole public revenue is in most countries employed in maintaining unproductive hands. Such are the people who compose a numerous and splendid court, a great ecclesiastical establishment, great fleets and armies. . . . Such people, as they themselves produce nothing, are all maintained by the product of other men's labor. . . . When multiplied therefore to an unnecessary number, they may in a particular year consume so great a share of this produce as not to leave a sufficiency for maintaining the productive labourers, who will reproduce it next year. The next year's produce, therefore, will be less than that of the foregoing, and, if the same disorder should continue, that of the third year will be less than that of the second."[7]

On public debt: For Adam Smith, money borrowed by government was "from the moment in which the lenders advanced it, a certain portion of the annual production of wealth, turned away from serving as capital to serve as revenue; from maintaining productive labors, to maintaining unproductive ones; and to be spent and wasted, generally in the course of the year, without even the hope of any further reproductions. . . . Had they [the lenders] not made their loans to the government, there would have been in the country twice as much capital, two portions of the annual produce, instead of one, employed in maintaining productive labor."[8]

As a spokesman for constraining the public household in the same manner as the private, Adam Smith acknowledged that fluctuations in economic activity would occur, biasing the economy sometimes toward recession, sometimes toward inflationary prosperity. But at the same time, he found self-correcting forces in a free, competitive market that would operate to restore a balance, if permitted to do so. He called these balancing forces the "invisible hand."

Government's role, then, was simply to avoid adding more instability to the economy through its own profligacy. By keeping debt and taxes low it should promote thrift and saving, both indispensable ingredients for achieving the "wealth of nations."

It was this position to which John Maynard Keynes took deep exception.

JOHN MAYNARD KEYNES

Thought fellow Britishers and economists, John Maynard Keynes and Adam Smith had few things in common, and those were superficial. Born 160 years apart, Smith in 1723 and Keynes in 1883, they were both educated in England's best universities, Smith at Oxford and Keynes at Cambridge. Both taught in universities, Keynes at his alma mater and Smith at Glasgow. Both left academic life, Keynes to serve illustriously in government service and Smith to travel and fill his notebooks with thoughts and observations about commerce and trade. Smith returned home to write *The Wealth of Nations,* while Keynes returned to Cambridge, where, as an "academic scribbler," he wrote *The General*

Theory of Employment, Interest, and Money. Though each wrote other significant books, their enduring fame rests on those singular titles.

Whatever similarities there were end there, for their economic views were poles apart. In fact, it would be fair to say that whatever one asserted the other refuted. Take, for example, Smith's contention that "what is prudent in the conduct of every family can scarce be folly in that of a great kingdom." Keynes denied it, in fact turning Smith's assertion about-face to say, in effect, that management practices that may be folly in a family will indeed be prudent in the affairs of a great state.

Their contrary views on public debt illustrate the point. Smith, taking the private household as a model, abhorred public debt, but Keynes embraced it as a cure for recessions and high unemployment. Recessions, he argued, are caused by shrinking demand for goods and services. So the government should deliberately go into debt during recessions, spending massively to create jobs and restore buying power and hence demand.

Smith was skeptical of such notions. Massive government spending only transfers productive capital into unproductive hands, he contended. The result is to cripple even more the ability of the private economy to employ people.

Keynes discounted that risk. Debts will not become permanent, he promised. As full employment returns, so will tax dollars to the public treasury. Debts will be paid off from the surplus, and more money will be available for productive purposes.

But public debts don't get paid off, Smith would have countered. Said he: "When national debts have once been accumulated to a certain degree there is scarcely, I believe, a single instance of their having been fairly and completely paid off."

Keynes had no such doubts. The basis of his confidence was his trust in economic planners. A small group of highly skilled economists, no doubt members of the intellectual aristocracy like himself, would guide the government in both its borrowing and its paying back. Under their engineering the economy would be alternately expanded during periods of recession and contracted during periods of prosperity. Paying off the debt during prosperity would curb excessive spending and dampen the fires or inflation. Expansion during recession would restore jobs and demand. Thus the principle of the balanced budget would not be destroyed but only lengthened from a single budget year to the period of the business cycle, perhaps three or four. The effect would be to stabilize the economy and level out its gyrations between boom and bust.

Smith, on the other hand, was suspicious of economic engineers. The economy, he believed, was an intricate, infinitely complex interlinked web, and tampering with any strand would risk disrupting the others. Men's efforts to manipulate the economy only created more havoc. As I said previously, he had more faith in the "invisible hand" of free competition.

Who won the great debate? That is hard to say; it still rages on. Initially, one factor definitely favored Keynes, the year his *General Theory* appeared. It was 1936, the pit of the Great Depression. No one in living memory could remember a depression of such severity and grinding hardship. Adam Smith's "invisible hand" was indeed invisible. The unfettered market made no effort to correct its deep ills. There was no wage low enough to provide employment and keep men out of breadlines. There were no prices low enough to create demand for goods and services. There was no money. No one of Smith's persuasion had an answer. But Keynes did: Spend! And so the politicians did. The time-honored norm of a balanced budget was jettisoned, lavish borrowing came into vogue, and savings became imprudent.

DID KEYNES MISJUDGE HUMAN NATURE?

The revolution that Keynes wrought did not take place overnight, however, for it began on a modest scale and was directed at only one segment of society — the poor. Its purpose was to get them off the dole and out of the breadlines and return them to a life of decency and dignity. Their claims upon the public household were deemed by most people to be reasonable and just.

But almost unnoticed a historic watershed had been reached, and there was no turning back. As the years passed, the poor were not the only ones making claims upon the state. The middle and upper classes now reached out for their largess, not to satisfy their necessities, but their wants. Rising expectations gave way to widening demands for rising "entitlements," guarantees of the good life for all. Ushered in was the age of the Great Society.

Ushered in also was the age of the enterprising politicians. Cut off from the restraints of the balanced budget, they were set free to manipulate expenditures for political purposes. Constituencies expanded wonderfully. Once confined to wooing the poor by providing necessities, they could now woo everybody else by appealing to their wants. Forgotten was Keynes's advice about paying back in good times what had been borrowed in bad. Forgotten, too, was Aristotle's warning about wants being "insatiable" and therefore "unnatural." As a consequence, the public household's debts mounted up, and at a frightful cost to the private households. Inflation skyrocketed, and purchasing power plummeted. The Great Society was becoming a great delusion. What had gone wrong?

If the prominence of Keynes rested in part in the timing of his *General Theory,* his failure rested in naive and erroneous assumptions about the psychology of political behavior.[9] Primarily, there were two. Keynes assumed that future governments would be directed by an elite group of skilled and disinterested economic planners, who, rising above self-interests, would alternately contract and expand the economy upon demand. "Fine tuning," he called it, and he assumed that the politicians would be like pliant putty in the planners' hands, forsaking their natural instincts to overspend. In both assumptions he turned out to be wrong.

Keynes's biographer, Sir Ray Harrod, seemed to have sensed his subject's vulnerability in making these assumptions. Said he: "If owing to the needs of planning, the functions of government became very far reaching and multifarious, would it be possible for the aristocracy to remain in essential control? Keynes tended to the end to think of the really important decisions being reached by a small group of intelligent people. . . . But would not a democratic government having a wide multiplicity of duties tend to get out of control and act in a way of which the intelligent did not approve?"[10]

It apparently never occurred to Keynes that the self-interests of politicians might run exactly contrary to the planners, that by nature they are out to please their constituents, and that the results would be disastrous deficits that, as Adam Smith had warned, would never be paid off. Keynes apparently had little awareness that survival is the first law of politics, even when it runs counter to the public interest. He blithely assumed that political survival is enhanced by following the ruling elite. He seemed ignorant of the fact that the political survival requires adherence, instead, to the presumptions of the political marketplace.

It is in their understanding of political psychology that the gulf between Adam Smith and John Maynard Keynes becomes most apparent. Adam Smith began with a healthy dose of skepticism about the motivations of rulers. He expected them to be irresponsible spendthrifts, piling up debt that they had no intention of paying off. He warned of their great power to destroy the economy, if it were to their political advantage. If the economy is to flourish, he asserted, it would be in spite of the rulers, not because of them. They constituted a burden that a free economy had to learn to carry.

Keynes, on the other hand, assumed that politicians are farsighted individuals who act as trustees of the future. But Smith knew that for them only the present is certain. They cannot forgo short-term popularity for long-term gains. In politics immediate credit is all that counts, even if taking it threatens to endanger the future.

Keynes apparently died believing that should politicians not follow his principles, the elite like himself could easily appeal over their heads to the people and set matters straight. F. A. Hayek, who visited with Keynes shortly before his death, spoke of the latter's confidence in his powers of persuasion. "I asked him whether he was not getting alarmed about the use to which some of his disciples were putting his theories. His reply was that these theories had been greatly needed in the 1930s, but that if these theories should ever become harmful, I could be assured that he would quickly bring about a change in public opinion."[11]

A few weeks after this revealing discussion, John Maynard Keynes suffered a severe heart attack and died. Unawares, he had created a new environment in which was discovered a new political alchemy: how borrowed dollars could be transformed into electoral gold.

SUMMARY

To give human nature its due has been the purpose of these first three essays, to see human nature not at the margin of politics but as its central power and determining force. Historical thought assigns it that role, so, too, contemporary behavioral psychology. The effect is to de-intellectualize the political process and also the debt. The latter is not a reasoned investment in rationally arrived at economic goals. It is, instead, the accumulated dollar costs over more than a half-century of meeting the displaced needs and wants of untold numbers of incumbent congressmen who found it politically advantageous to borrow and too politically risky to tax. They were doing what came naturally. And that was made legitimate by the miscalculations of John Maynard Keynes. Would we be in our current fiscal predicament had we taken more seriously the views of Aristotle and Adam Smith? The question is academic, of course, but the chances are the answer would be no.

To this point in the book certain propositions about human nature and politics have been suggested, their history briefly sketched, and different views about them debated. With this as background, I turn now to the main business at hand: the political psychology of the debt.

II PSYCHOLOGICAL ROOTS OF THE DEBT

4   The Anatomy of Political Desire

> He who is active in politics strives for power either as a means in serving other ends, ideal or egoistic, or as power for power's sake, that is in order to enjoy the prestige feeling that power gives.
>
> — Max Weber

Political desire, I suggested in the introduction, is the driving force behind the debt. In this essay I explore the psychological and sociological anatomy of that desire. My view is that it has its origin in two sources: the internalized needs and wants of the members of Congress and the conditions of their lives as professional politicians. After exploring those, I shall note how deficit spending satisfies each, and quite admirably. It "becomes" their natures, I conclude, while taxing does not. That is why Congress taxes only in cases of fiscal extremes, when the body politic rejects further borrowing.

Before proceeding to the main tasks, however, a further word should be said about the particular region of behavior being explored. It is a region largely unseen, cut off from public view, where the primordial forces of human nature play. It is that area of the behavioral iceberg that, though beneath the surface, really explains what is seen above. Sociologist Robert Merton called these seen and unseen levels of behavior manifest and latent, and his comments about them are instructive for our purposes here.

MANIFEST AND LATENT BEHAVIOR

In his *Social Theory and Social Structure* Merton defined manifest behavior as the visible part: it is open and subject to public review.[1]

Latent behavior, by contrast, is mostly hidden from public scrutiny, arising as it does in inner needs and wants.

It is Merton's further distinction, however, that is most relevant to our inquiry: *Only invisible, latent behavior can explain why people do what they do.* Public, manifest behavior is but a distorted image of it. Thus to understand behavior, fiscal or otherwise, go to its sources, not its blurred reflection.

To illustrate his distinction Merton cited the two levels of behavior of those big-city political machines of earlier times. What the public saw of them was the manifest level, mostly unsavory, including such practices as patronage, bossism, and the outright buying of votes. And for these political malpractices the machines were roundly censured by political reformers. But this criticism could not explain why the machines came into being in the first place or what kept them going. The answer to that was to be found in their latent behavior, such as providing food for the hungry, jobs for the jobless, and help for the sick and dispossessed. The machines flourished because they met basic human needs and wants. When they faded away it was because those needs and wants came to be satisfied in other ways, not because of the moral ridicule.

For years, members of Congress have been roundly censured for their deficit spending, but that did not reduce the debt. In fact, it had the opposite effect. The reason can only be discovered by inquiring into their unseen latent behavior, where human nature and politics consort to satisfy basic needs and wants. It is that arena of behavior on which this essay concentrates.

BASIC HUMAN NEEDS AND WANTS

As indicated in the previous essay, the origin and the character of human drives have been subject of longtime discussion and debate. In our time, the matter has been pursued vigorously by behavioral psychologists, and not without varied results. There is a convergence of opinion, however, about the main wellsprings of human action. And this convergence is clearly shown in the various lists of "drives," "traits," and "needs" — the terminology varies — produced by scholars of human behavior.

One of the best known of these lists is that of Abraham Maslow.[2] In his massive *Motivation and Personality* Maslow identifies a hierarchy of basic needs and wants, five in number, which range from the purely biological up through the highest social needs. It is this hierarchical concept that sets Maslow's list off from some others. He sees needs and wants as progressive, with the satisfaction of one leading to the emergence of the next.

Those needs and wants, according to Maslow, are:

> physiological needs,
> safety needs,
> the need for love,
> the need for esteem, and
> the need for self-actualization.

Here, in brief, is the way this psychologist described those five basic needs.

Physiological Needs

From physiological needs spring the drives to eat, to engage in sex, to sleep, to exercise, and to participate in sports.

Safety Needs

When physiological needs are gratified, the safety needs emerge. They drive humans to seek "security, protection, and freedom from fear." The need for safety also has broad social implications. It causes persons to seek structure and order in their lives. Maslow generalized that "the average child, and, less obviously, the average adult, in our society generally prefers a safe, orderly, predictable, lawful, organized world which he can count on and in which unexpected, unmanageable, chaotic, and other dangerous things do not happen."

THE NEED FOR LOVE

The need for love, Maslow found, is a derivative of the need for safety. He observed that modern society denies love, leading to anxiety, tension, and the frantic search for love substitutes. This denial of love, he said, accounts for the rapid increase of "personal growth groups" and "intentional communities." They are in part motivated by "the unsatisfied hunger for intimacy, for belongingness and by the need to overcome the widespread feeling of aloneness."

THE NEED FOR ESTEEM

The need for esteem, Maslow judged, is an almost universal drive and has two parts. One is "the desire for strength, for achievement, for adequacy, for mastery and competence, for confidence in the face of the world, and for independence and freedom." The other part is "the desire for reputation or prestige, status, fame and glory, dominance, recognition, attention, importance, dignity or appreciation."

The satisfaction of the need for esteem leads on to feelings of self-confidence, worth, and adequacy, but the denial of esteem "produces feelings of inferiority, of weakness, and helplessness."

THE NEED FOR SELF-ACTUALIZATION

Self-actualization stands at the top of Maslow's hierarchy of basic needs and wants. "Even if all these [other] needs are satisfied," he asserted, "we may still often [if not always] expect that a new discontent and restlessness will soon develop, unless the individual is doing what he, individually, is fitted for . . . what a man *can* be he *must* be. He must be true to his own nature."

In sum, our needs and wants begin in biological demands and end in social achievements that best express the individual self. In between, the need for a safe, orderly, and predictable environment and the need for love, esteem, status, reputation, recognition, dominance, and attention define the way we are in our motivational makeups.

Do the needs and wants of congressmen and congresswomen differ from those of nonpolitical types? The evidence indicates that they do, not in kind, but in emphasis and intensity. Consider next the differences between political and nonpolitical personalities.

POLITICAL PERSONALITIES:
THEIR NEEDS AND WANTS

Early political scientists saw little point in investigating the role of personality in political affairs. Even Arthur F. Bentley, regarded by many as the patron saint of political science, eschewed such study. In the first chapter of *The Process of Government* (1908), he dismissed turn-of-the-century psychology as "catch phrases and verbal toys."[3] And as for the then current theory of motivation, he wrote it off as "soul stuff." "It is a vicious circle," he proclaimed, "which begins in a rough untested guess, and comes out with a rough, untested guess, with nothing but metaphysics in between."

There are likely a host of reasons for the slowness in recognizing that politically inclined persons have some different motivational characteristics and that these may help to account for their decisions and behavior. Like Bentley, many persons may simply reject the idea that inner motivations have anything to do with political behavior. In other words, "what you see is what you get." But if one asks politicians in private, where confidentiality is assured, why they are in politics, it becomes quickly apparent that what you see is not what you get. Conventional answers like "I want to make a difference" are not the real reasons at all. Many politicians, in fact, find that question very hard to answer; one can see them digging deep within. "It's in my blood, I guess," or some variation of that, is the way the response is apt to come out, testimony to the deeper motivations that lie within.

Another reason may be that inquiry into political motivations requires a quite different way of viewing public figures than we are used to. We usually deal with them only in their manifest roles, say as information givers, decision makers, and/or power brokers. Official relationships, however, do not reveal latent behavior. To get at that matter one needs to go beneath formal roles, and that means practiced observation or, better still, systematic research designed for the purpose.

A third reason is that we do not take seriously the warning of Graham Wallas and Walter Lippmann about overintellectualizing politics. We pay too much attention to the public pronouncements of politicians and too little to the personal reasons they make them. This does not mean that such pronouncements are not sincerely made. It does mean, however, that public utterances should not be confused with private motivations.

Turn now to the question at hand: What particular needs and wants drive politicians? The evidence indicates that they are those we associate with power, like dominance, importance, fame, glory, status, esteem, prestige, recognition, and attention. For shorthand, I shall refer to this collection of needs and wants as the "power syndrome."

That power is central to politics is, of course, an idea as old as politics itself, and many there are who have discoursed upon the subject. But few, I believe, have described the role of power in political behavior better than Max Weber, the German-born economist and sociologist. In his lecture on politics as a vocation, an excerpt from which is quoted at the beginning of this essay, he asserted that power was the key need and want of politicians. Those active in politics strive for it, he said, either as a way of serving "ideal or egoistic" aims or simply for the "prestige feeling that power gives."

Power, Weber asserted, is one of the "inner enjoyments" of a political career. "The knowledge of influencing men, of participating in power over them, and above all, the feeling of holding in one's hand a nerve fiber of historically important events can elevate the professional politician above everyday routine even when he is placed in formally modest positions."[5]

Weber credited the strength of the power need among politicians to the character of the state itself and its foundation in force. "We have to say," he wrote, "that a state is a human community that [successfully] claims the monopoly of the legitimate use of physical force within a given territory. . . . Hence politics for us means striving to influence the distribution of power either among states or among groups within a state."[6]

SOCIAL SCIENCE RESEARCH ON POLITICAL PERSONALITY

Research tends to confirm the importance of the power syndrome to politically inclined persons. It also takes us beyond Weber's generalization to the particulars of how the power syndrome works in actual practice. Here are three examples.

How self-image figures in the decision to become a political candidate was the subject of James Barber's research.[7] He found that it did play an important part, and in two quite different ways. Taking as his research population first-term legislators in the Connecticut House of Representatives, Barber discovered that those few who came with high self-images did so precisely for this reason. The experience apparently fulfilled the high images of self. But the others, and they were many, came to have their low self-images raised. Wrote Barber of this majority group:

Our hypothesis must be that they are attracted to politics by forces strong enough to overcome all objections they are aware of. Politics must offer them personal rewards that offset the strains involved. . . . On the motivational side such deep reaching appeals are very likely linked to self esteem, to the fundamental need such people feel for getting and confirming self esteem. As we have seen, political office holding can offer some strong and specific rewards to the damaged self, bolstering up the ego here, offering an extra chance there, conferring a moral blessing in another place. These rewards may compensate for much of the embarrassment, frustration, and confusion the unconfident person experiences in stepping into politics. From among the politically available such attractions may entice candidates who are

not socially active or whose social activities are inadequate compensation for
their needs.[8]

"Political candidacy appears, then, as a form of deviant behavior,"
Barber concluded, "drawing toward it exceptional people — exceptional
either in their high abilities, or in their strong needs. Our tentative
estimate regarding self-esteem must be that elected officials possess either
rather high or low levels of self esteem compared with other persons who
have the same social characteristics."[9]

Rufus Browning and Herbert Jacob sought to find out how strongly
politicians are motivated to seek power and achievement and how different communities might affect that quest differently.[10] They compared
politicians with nonpoliticians in an eastern city and Louisiana parishes.
The two research sites differed sharply in both the economic and political
opportunities they offered potential candidates. In the eastern city there
were no restrictions "on power and achievement opportunities" offered
politically inclined individuals. The researchers reported: "Expectations
are prevalent that it is possible to go on to the state legislative office or
higher from the position of councilman or mayor."

At the same time, the eastern city was depressed economically and
therefore offered few opportunities in business and industry for power-
and achievement-oriented persons. Economic opportunities were further
"restricted by the exclusion of several immigrant minority groups from
the highest positions in industry and finance." By contrast, the Louisiana
parishes offered many economic but few political opportunities. As a
result, "plentiful opportunities for power and achievement in the economic arena channelled strongly motivated men into economic rather than
political activity." Concurrently, parish politics was "factional, frag-
mented, shifting, and personal, making political mobility upward to state
or national offices . . . practically unheard of."

On the basis of their research, Browning and Jacob concluded that
"simply being a politician does not in itself entail a distinctive concern for
power or achievement, as indicated by the fact that in the Louisiana
parishes such persons were drawn to economic enterprise rather than
running for office." But in communities where politics and political
issues are at the center of attention (as in the eastern city) "men attracted
to politics are likely to be more power and achievement oriented than in
communities where politics commands only peripheral interest."

The summary observations of Browning and Jacob support the
connection between personality traits and political behavior. "The implications of data of this sort are not trivial," they conclude. "Groups of men

who differ with respect to these traits will run a government in sharply different ways. . . . It is here that the significance of data on personality is apparent, in the decisions of political leaders, in the yielding to certain pressures, and not to others, in their acceptance of some decision promises over others. Information on the motives of politicians provides us with links between complex social, economic, and political variables, on the one hand, and the patterns of recruitment and behavior of leaders, on the other."[11]

The third research project is the most comprehensive of the three, since it included a large number of legislators, in Congress and out, and in foreign countries as well. James L. Payne and four colleagues explored this paradox: Why, when politics as a vocation is stressful and taxing and hardly anyone's idea of a cushy, comfortable position, is the supply of candidates so copious?[12] "Clearly," the researchers hypothesized, "individuals are not attracted to politics by ordinary human pleasures. What, then, does attract them?"

As a result of their extensive interviewing over a period of five years, 1964–69, Payne et al. found it necessary to modify some of their original conceptions about the motivation of legislators.

> There was a natural tendency — which we shared — to approach the motivation issue by looking for specific goals, reasons, or purposes. Thus we are disposed to say that A is in politics "to help the poor," or B is in politics "to promote the peaceful uses of atomic energy." Empirically, when one gets a close look at politicians, the proposition that they participate for intellectual "reasons" or carry out some specific goal simply will not stand up. . . . Instead, we discovered, it was an emotional type drive that propelled individuals to accept the rigors of political life.[13]

In their extensive interviewing, the interest of Payne and colleagues was drawn particularly to legislators with a status incentive, those with the need for "prestige or public recognition." They reported that the number of status types in the U.S. House of Representatives "apparently increased substantially from the mid 1950's." The reason was "a change in the system of selecting congressmen. The recruitment system became more 'democratic' during this period. Both primary and general elections were opened up. Gone were the bosses and party machines that controlled nominations and elections: candidates were more often left to fend for themselves in strenuous mass popularity contests."[14]

This increase in status types, the researchers observed, accounted for subsequent changes in the House of Representatives. "For example, the publicity-seeking impulse of status types helps account for the increase in the number of floor speeches, for the growth in newsletters, TV taping facilities, and congressional PR staff; for the full admission of broadcast media into committee meeting hearings in the late 1960's; for the virtual disappearance of closed door hearings in the 1970's; and for the rise in attention getting, scandal oriented committee hearings."[15]

In summarizing their research, Payne and colleagues concluded that "status types are likely to enact measures that are popularly appealing but counter productive in the long run." They placed deficit spending in this category.

> Perhaps the most common theme of governmental mismanagement around the world lies in the fiscal and monetary realm. It is superficially appealing to issue governmental benefits to the populace and superficially appealing not to raise taxes to pay for such benefits. The shortsighted handling of fiscal affairs leads, then, to bankruptcy or monetary debasement and inflation. The economic difficulties cause, in turn, social conflict and hostility directed at government. . . . Politics is a gong show. The stage is open to any member of the audience to do his thing. It is personality that governs why some people seek to be on stage, and it is personality that determines the kind of act they put on. If we seek to understand this spectacle, we must explore the personalities of the participants.[16]

The work of persons like Max Weber and contemporary social science researchers allows us to conclude that the power syndrome among politicians is alive, well, and influential. It must be taken into account when inquiring into what politicians do and why they do it.

In concluding this psychological look at political desires, and before turning to the sociological aspects of the matter, I should make explicit something that to this point has been only implicit. The unspoken assumption has been that private needs and wants somehow get satisfied through public political activity. But, psychologically speaking, how? And what new perspectives does the psychological explanation provide on congressional behavior? I shall consider those questions next.

HOW PRIVATE NEEDS AND WANTS ARE SATISFIED THROUGH POLITICS

This matter cannot be considered without reference to the pioneering work of political scientist Harold Lasswell. Lasswell began as a student at the University of Chicago under Charles E. Merriam, himself an early advocate of the study of personality in politics. Following an unconventional career path, Lasswell became a professor of law at Yale, from which position he specialized in the application of Freudian psychology to politics. Selected titles from his books and articles reveal the direction of his work: *Psychopathology and Politics* (1930),[17] *Power and Personality* (1948),[18] "Effect of Personality on Political Participation" (1954), and *Politics: Who Gets What, When and How* (1958).[19]

Lasswell developed the thesis that the leap from private desires to public satisfaction through politics is best explained by the psychological concept of displacement. Displacement occurs when private desires, frustrated in their fulfillment in the primary environment, are attached to public objects and causes, the better to achieve their satisfaction. Thus basic human needs and wants do not change, only the venue for realizing them. Political actions are, in effect, displaced private desires.

Lasswell put it this way: "The fully developed political type works out his destiny in the name of the public good. He displaces private motives on public objects in the name of the public good."[20] Lasswell goes on:

> The true politician learns to use the world of public objects as a means of alleviating the stresses of his intimate environment. Cravings for deference, frustrated or overindulged in the intimate circle, find expression in the secondary environment. This displacement is legitimized in the name of plausible symbols. He does not act for the sake of action; he implies that he strives for the glory of God, the sanctity of the home, the independence of the nation, the emancipation of the class. In the extreme case the politician is bound to no specific objects in his environment. . . . He is concerned only with the deference meanings of objects of his ego.[21]

The far-reaching implications of Lasswell's thesis have not escaped the reader. They are several in number. The first corroborates Merton's claim about the key importance of the latent aspects of behavior. It is that in every public political act, like deficit spending, there is encased a private human desire. Read this way, public, manifest political behavior should not be taken literally. It is for public consumption. It should be considered, instead, within the context of politicians' private needs and wants. Those are what inform the fiscal message.

Another closely related implication is that public acts, such as deficit financing, are not performed for their own sake or because they possess particular merit. They are done, instead, because they hold the prospect of fulfilling certain personal desires. Thus the act of deficit spending is incidental to the real reasons for doing it. It satisfies some urgent private need or want, or it would not be done.

The third implication follows from the second. The state is the prize of political struggle, the object of which makes the realization of private needs and wants possible. The state has no inherent value except as a public means to a private end; it is incidental to the main objective. Thus one would not expect that what politicians do would necessarily strengthen the state; they may just as easily weaken it.

How should Lasswell's thesis be judged? Does it describe some congressmen, many, most, or none at all? The evidence presented by the social science research just cited suggests that the answer ranges somewhere between many and most, but certainly not all. Some able members simply do not fit Lasswell's model of deference-dependent human beings who are drawn to Congress to bolster their battered self-images. Their own inner resources are strong, their self-images confident. Had they chosen to stay in private life, they likely would have made it to the top in whatever they chose to do. But Lasswell's main thrust is borne out by research: For many members Congress is a stepping-stone to status, recognition, attention, dominance, and reputation.

LIFE AS A PROFESSIONAL POLITICIAN

In the introduction I observed that since Congress "is now composed almost entirely of career politicians dependent upon holding onto their seats for both their livelihoods and psychic satisfactions . . . [it would be necessary] to examine with some care the connection between a deep personal investment in a congressional seat and fiscal behavior." In this section the sociological meanings of that investment are explored.

In a democracy large numbers of people engage in political activity in one form or another, but relatively few make a career of it. People vote, follow politics in the media, argue about it, write letters to the editor and their member of Congress, contribute money, participate in local caucuses, act as precinct captains and poll watchers, serve on boards and commissions, and become delegates to county, state, and national conventions. Of this large number, however, only a limited few ever run for and hold office with the intent of making a living at it.

In sociological terms, what is the difference between these two groups? And do these differences affect political behavior?

LIVING FOR AND OFF POLITICS

In his lecture on politics as a vocation cited earlier, Max Weber made a distinction between living for and off politics, and he called that distinction "a substantial aspect of the matter." Weber put it this way:

There are two ways of making politics one's vocation. Either one lives "for" politics or one lives "off" politics. By no means is this distinction an exclusive one. The rule is, rather, that man does both, at least in thought, and certainly he does both in practice. He who lives "for" politics makes politics his life, in an internal sense. Either he enjoys the naked possession of power he exerts, or he nourishes his inner balance and self-feeling by the consciousness that his life has *meaning* in the service of a "cause." In this internal sense, every sincere man who lives for a cause also lives off the cause. The distinction hence refers to a more substantial aspect of the matter, economic. He who strives to make politics a permanent *source of income* lives "off" politics as a vocation, whereas he who does not do this lives "for" politics.[22]

Just how "substantial" a consideration in behavioral terms is this striving "to make politics a permanent source of income"? Since it requires that every political issue be weighed in terms of the next election, it is obviously very substantial. Consciously or not, the preferred courses of action come to be those most likely to win votes. Proposals come to be judged not for their inherent worth, but for their political utility.

A second difference arises in the norms society applies to those who live for and off politics. Politics as an avocation is valued in our democracy. The citizen politician who gives up evenings and weekends to do political chores usually finds support for his activities in the community. He is doing his "civic duty." He need not apologize for it; indeed, he finds his self-image enhanced by it.

Further, this positive norm is encouraged from childhood onward. In family, church, and school the child learns that voting is the "right thing to do," that "keeping up on the issues of the day" is important, and that a good citizen "participates." Even if, as an adult, that person does no more than vote, that minimal act is thought of as commendable.

By contrast, living off politics invokes a negative set of norms. While the holding of some offices, especially high ones, is accorded certain deference and respect, running for and holding office generally is not regarded as "normal" in the same sense that voting and volunteering are normal. "Should one vote?" always elicits an unqualified "yes." "Should one live off politics?" however, is likely to invoke a frown and: "What's the matter? Can't he make a living at anything else?"

This negative norm, also, is learned at an early age. Children soon learn that politics has its "dirty" side, operating by "deals," and that being on the public payroll is viewed by some cartoonists as "feeding at the public trough." So, while the citizen politician has his self-image bolstered by his activities, the career politician may well have his battered. And that suggests the third aspect of the matter.

Ambiguity marks the position of the politician who lives off politics, and this ambiguity has far-reaching ramifications. Not only is his position discounted by prevailing norms; constitutional democracy makes his job dispensable. Democracy's core idea is that no one is indispensable. As a result, the career politician's job is never fully secure; it is always in jeopardy. If Maslow was correct in placing man's safety needs high on the list, those who live off politics must work doubly hard to achieve these needs. Every election places their jobs squarely on the line.

Added to the dispensable nature of the job are its inherent stresses and strains. Not least among them are those of getting the job in the first place. Few jobs require more hassle to get than elective office. The rigors entailed in campaigning, traveling about, raising money, constantly putting on a good face, forever rebutting the opponent, watching the polls for political signs, and the endless need to be politically swift of foot make securing even the toughest private-sector job look easy by comparison.

Moreover, these stresses and strains only intensify with victory. The atmosphere of the congressional workplace is usually marked by tension, and frequently acrimony, masked over by a thin veneer of ritualistic politeness. And yet even political enemies must be tolerated and worked with: One day they may be needed for a favor.

The legislative work load is heavy, and the number of measures and issues to be understood is far beyond the capacity of even a miracle worker. For this reason the members have no alternative but to turn for help to staff, fellow legislators, constituents, and lobbyists. The resulting dependency can rankle. "Am I getting good advice?" "Will my opponent use my lack of personal understanding against me on the campaign trail?" "Will I be sorry that I didn't dig into the matter myself?" These questions can be unnerving.

Though frequently dependent on others for knowledge and advice, congressional members are still solely responsible for their own political fates. There was a time in our political history when they could count on substantial help, financial and otherwise, from their political parties. No longer. Now they must raise their own money, fight their own political battles, create their own constituencies, and get out their own votes on election day. Congress is, in effect, a collection of 535 autocracies, each fighting for its own survival.

To make matters worse, the constituency upon which the legislator's future depends is largely unseen. Most congressmen and congresswomen work far from home base. Some constituents they see face to face, of course, in their Washington or district offices, at church suppers, and service club luncheons, and in visits to union halls, malls, and other places where people gather. But these represent only a small portion of the voters they must depend on at election time. So no wonder they are harried by the fact that their constituents, when asked by pollsters, cannot even recall their names.

Now what kind of political behaviors are these conditions of life likely to produce? They may be described as entrepreneurial and highly symbolic.

Congressmen and Congresswomen as Political Entrepreneurs

Almost every psychological need and want and every sociological condition of life conspire to make incumbents political entrepreneurs. Strongly driven by desires associated with the power syndrome, they find themselves in a competitive political jungle designed to frustrate the fulfillment of practically every one of these desires. To survive and have even half a chance of finding Maslow's "self-actualization," they must become to politics what every businessman is to commerce and trade: an out-and-out entrepreneur. No one has described that reality better, I believe, than Joseph Schumpeter, the former Harvard economist of the Austrian School. In his insightful study of *Capitalism, Socialism, and Democracy,* Schumpeter defined the whole political role as the pursuit of office. He put the matter this way: "The man is still in the nursery who has not absorbed so as never to forget the saying attributed to one of our most successful politicians who ever lived: 'What businessmen do not understand is that just as they are dealing in oil so I am dealing in votes.'"[23]

What kind of political behavior does "dealing in votes" imply? It suggests behavior high in symbolism and meager in substantive content.

Political Behavior as Symbolism

The symbolic nature of political behavior is best understood in terms of what happens when entrepreneurial incumbents enter an institution that is better at frustrating their needs and wants than satisfying them. They must resort to symbolic behavior and cannot do otherwise, for the real actions of Congress are few and far between. The bureaucratic machinery of Congress is heavy and slow-moving. And its rules are just as apt to checkmate the incumbent's grand schemes to please his constituents as they are to expedite them. The actual work of Congress is decentralized in a maze of committees, each jealously guarding its legislative turf. The leadership of the institution, while powerful, is always constrained by the political needs of the members. In short, if the enterprising members had to wait for real reportable products to flow from the legislative machine, they would be waiting for much of their political lives.

But there is an answer, and a good one: Busy oneself with things that give the appearance of action. In his study *Congress: The Electoral Connection,* political scientist David Mayhew gives an excellent description of the symbolic behaviors of the members.[24] In introducing those behaviors Mayhew states: "I shall make a simple abstract assumption about human motivation and then speculate about the consequences of behavior based on that motivation. Specifically, I shall conjure up a vision of United States congressmen as single-minded seekers of reelection, see what kind of activity that goal implies, and then speculate about how congressmen so motivated are likely to go about building and sustaining institutions and making policy."[25]

The symbolic behaviors in which the members of Congress engage are, according to Mayhew, three in number.

First, they advertise. They engage "in any effort to disseminate one's name among constituents in such a fashion as to create a favorable image but in messages having little or no issue content. A successful congressman builds what amounts to a brand name. . . . The personal qualities to emphasize are experience, knowledge, responsiveness, concern, sincerity, independence, and the like."[26]

Second, they engage in credit claiming. They act "to generate a belief . . . that one is personally responsible for causing the government, or some unit thereof, to do something . . . desirable. The political logic of this, from the congressman's point of view, is that the actor (read voter) who believes that a member can make pleasing things happen will no doubt wish to keep him in office so that he can make pleasing things happen in the future."[27]

Finally, representatives engage in position taking. They make judgmental statements "on anything likely to be of interest to political actors. . . . The congressman as position taker is a speaker rather than a doer. The electoral requirement is not that he can make pleasing things happen but that he can make pleasing judgemental statements."[28]

In opening this essay I expressed the view that the fiscal excesses represented by the deficit arise in, and can be explained by, the internalized needs and wants of members of Congress and the conditions of their lives as professional politicians. I turn now to consider how these are admirably served by deficit spending and ill served by taxing.

IMPLICATIONS FOR THE DEFICIT

How, exactly, does borrowing satisfy incumbents' needs and wants? How does it "become" their condition of life? And why, politically speaking, do they find it preferable to taxing?

One way to gain an understanding of these questions is to compare and contrast borrowing by private citizens and the members of Congress in terms of rewards and punishments. The results will show that in the case of private citizens the rewards and punishments work to curb excessive debt, but with representatives to encourage it and explain why private debts tend to get paid off, while Congress-created debts do not.

Borrowing by Citizens

Like most borrowing, citizen borrowing is the act of postponing the costs of consumption in order to have it now. The new car can be driven while it is being paid for. By contrast, lending is the act of forgoing current consumption in order to have more later, the more being made possible by the interest earned. But the net effect for both borrower and lender, assuming the arrangement is fair and equitable, is mutual satisfaction, even though they achieve it in different ways.

Now cast this transaction in terms of its rewards and punishments. The rewards are clear. The borrower has the pleasure of driving the new car, the lender the satisfaction of watching his money grow. Clear, too, are the punishments. The borrower must make the payments or risk having the car repossessed. Nor is the lender punishment-proof. To earn interest he must forgo the principal. He must also take the risk of losing some or all of it should the borrower default.

What is psychologically significant about this straightaway business arrangement is that both parties are constrained by the same hard reality: *The rewards are not punishment-free.* The pleasures of owning the new car are constrained by the need to make payments. The pleasures of earning interest are offset by the need to forgo the principal and assume certain risks. Neither borrower nor lender can have his or her cake and eat it, too. And because they cannot, they are encouraged to behave in a fiscally responsible way. In the language of learning psychology, good behavior is "reinforced" by rewards and discouraged by the threat of punishment.

There is far more to this illustration than psychological reality, of course. There is a supreme social reality. In the good society, freedom to enjoy is always constrained by responsibility. Indeed, there is no freedom without responsibility, only anarchy, freedom run amok. And societies remain free only to the degree that citizens, in government and out, feel bound by the necessity to be responsible.

What happens when they do not feel so bound? An example is the savings and loan debacle. Rewards became uncoupled from punishments, and fiscal excesses were the result. In insuring depositors against loss, in and of itself a caring act, Congress unwittingly weakened the psychological constraints that are present in all healthy business transactions. Insured against loss, however, depositors had no reason to be wary of management. Why worry? If the thrift failed, the government would pay.

Thus, from the very outset, the deposit insurance program weakened a key factor in honest business dealings: the keen and wary eyes of customers. Indeed, it might be said to put them to sleep. And what was the effect on the managers of savings and loans? Since a third party, rather than them personally, had insured their depositors against loss, they were free to become financial entrepreneurs, rather than the custodial agents of other people's money. So they plunged into the junk bond market and shaky real estate deals, knowing that the personal rewards could be handsome. At the same time, if the deals turned sour, only the faceless taxpayers would be hurt. The managers could have their cake and eat it, too.

And how about the members of Congress? They could also. Having insured their constituent-depositors against loss, they were free to yield to the high-pressure appeals of S and L lobbyists to expand their banking domains and relax stringent curbs on lending. The political payoffs were substantial, the money payoffs, too, in the form of campaign contributions. But what if the S and Ls failed? Not to worry. The members of Congress could then ride as white knights to the rescue, at the taxpayers' expense, of course.

Might the savings and loan debacle have been averted, or at least scaled down, had the rewards been constrained by the threat of punishment? More specifically, might depositors have been more wary had they had to assume some risk of losing their money? Might managers have been more prudent had they and their boards of directors been required personally to absorb some of the risks of loss? And would political entrepreneurs have been less solicitous of shaky S and Ls had their constituent-depositors also been at risk?

We shall never know for sure; we can only speculate. But the human tendencies seem clear: Had the rewards been constrained by the sure knowledge of the possibility of punishment, the results might have been very different.

Borrowing by Congressmen

First, a supreme irony. Few things congressmen do hold greater potential for harm for citizens than excessive borrowing to finance the ordinary costs of government. This liens citizens' future earnings and those of their children and grandchildren. It carries a constant threat of inflation. It raises interest rates and thereby keeps some citizens from buying a new home or starting a new business. While large infusions of borrowed money initially stimulate the economy, the long-term effect is to depress it. And that means fewer new jobs and higher unemployment. No doubt these are some of the reasons that one cannot find in today's public discourse a single serious defender of the deficit.

The irony? In spite of this great potential for harm, there are few things congressmen do that are punished so slightly or rewarded so politically handsomely as excessive borrowing. Consider why.

First, borrowing, as indicated before in another connection, takes place in an atmosphere of relative political safety, and especially in contrast to taxation. Borrowing has become so routine that, politically speaking, it is almost a nonevent. As it can be done quietly, by simply a vote to raise the debt ceiling, most citizens are unaware that it is happening. Some incumbents, of course, always use the occasion to posture against the deficit in order to impress voters back home, but how they will vote in the end is seldom in doubt. The money comes flowing back in, and spending can go on as usual. No fuss, no bother, no political cost.

A new tax proposal, by contrast, inevitably stirs up political hornets. A raucous public affair, it attracts every interest group, most of the media, and hopping mad citizens. For members of Congress it is a no-win situation, and the only way to cut the political losses is to make the new tax as inoffensive to powerful groups as possible and hide it as much as possible.

Would incumbents borrow less and tax more if the situation were reversed, if taxing could be done quietly and if borrowing exposed them to political punishment? Again, one must fall back on human tendencies. They suggest that would be the result.

Second, members of Congress borrow because the political rewards are immediate, whereas in taxing only the punishments are. With the extra money that borrowing produces, old constituent groups can be kept in the fold, new ones coaxed in, and others wooed closer. Requests for political favors can usually be answered with "Yes," but without those extra dollars, the answer might have to be a politically risky "No."

Third, a new tax always raises the specter of the high costs of government, while borrowing seldom does. In reality, of course, citizens never know their share of those costs or the price tag attached to various governmental   programs and services. Tax revenues flow into the Treasury on the basis of a graduated income tax and out again on the basis of political decisions. It is a system well designed to keep taxpayers in ignorance about any relationship between costs and benefits. But a new tax proposal inevitably raises the question of how cost-effective government really is, and that is a question incumbents would just as soon not touch, because it shifts the costs of government forward to an indefinite point in future time, whereas taxing assesses those costs immediately. In other words, some future congressman's constituents must pay, whereas, in taxing, *their* constituents must, and now.

Would incumbents be less eager to borrow if they could not shift the costs forward in time, if, say, they regularly had to send each constituent a bill for his or her share of the national debt, along with a notice, of course, about penalties for late payment? Who could doubt but that would have a sobering effect on excessive borrowing?

Finally, congressmen are not only exempt from repaying the debts they create; *they are also exempt from the ills that excessive debt itself creates*. Indeed, the matter can be taken one step further: Enterprising incumbents capitalize politically on such ills. Consider a few cases in point. High interest rates? Subsidized low rates to politically powerful groups pay off handsomely at the ballot box. High inflation? Entitlements can be made inflation-proof by tying them to the cost of living. Inflated rents? Subsidize them. Lagging businesses? Give them tax breaks and tariff protection.

The list could go on. What it comes down to is this: Probably no professional group in the United States is better able than the members of Congress to capitalize on the very problems they help to create. Were a medical doctor to spread contamination and then profit by cleaning it up, he would no doubt lose his license. But this possibility goes unexamined in the practice of congressional politics.

SUMMARY

The congressional power to borrow is more than fiscal, far more. It is the power to satisfy private needs and wants. It is the power to indulge those special urges to power associated with political personalities. If those are frustrated at the intimate level, it is the power to displace them on public objects and causes, in the name, of course, of the common good. It is the power to sidestep public scrutiny of fiscal affairs and thereby diminish representative democracy. It is the power to capitalize politically on the economic and social ills that excessive debt produces. Finally, it is the power to reject the alternative mode of financing government, taxing, because it can be politically damaging, even though its civic merits have much to recommend it. In short, this power, in practice, comes close to license.

Is there something about the nature of public money itself that encourages this license? That possibility is explored in the next essay.

5   The Political Psychology of Public Money

> The representative system of democracy is based ... on primitive exchange processes [and] suffers from numerous defects; one that illustrates its primitive character is that it depends too greatly on the political adroitness of men ... who are in effect like skillful professional traders in the barter economy.
>
> — James S. Coleman

In an evocative essay on the nature of political power, sociologist James Coleman likened it to money. Power is the medium of exchange in politics, he wrote. To emphasize the point he called power in politics "political money."[1]

In the essay Coleman compared political money with economic money. The idea of power as political money is old, he pointed out, going back, in the case of democracy, to ancient Greece and Rome. Yet as a medium of exchange power has evolved hardly at all. Still primitive, political money continues to depend upon the "political adroitness of men ... who are in effect like skillful professional traders in the barter economy." Who gets what is determined not by a uniform medium of exchange, but by skillful politicians who barter it away to the best political advantage.

The idea of economic money, also is old. But, by contrast with political money, economic money is highly evolved, standardized, and rational. Economic barter gave way long ago to commodity money such as gold and silver coins. Their value determined by weight, they served in exchange as uniform stores of value. Paper money, or notes, succeeded coins. Although they had no intrinsic value, they were promises to pay, backed by the full faith and credit of the issuer. Easily passed from hand to hand, paper money facilitated the growth of manufacturing, commerce, and trade.

Today's money is increasingly electronic. Untouched by human hands, it consists of obligations transferred by computers. Based on trust rather than adroit political manipulation, it permits instantaneous transactions between total strangers thousands of miles apart. The result is a highly sophisticated worldwide trade network that provides efficiently and reasonably well for the infinitely diverse economic needs of millions of people. By contrast, however, governmental needs are still served largely by barter, which depends upon skilled professional politicians as trader-mediators.

PUBLIC MONEY AS POLITICAL MONEY

Acknowledging my debt to Coleman, I propose in this essay to use his model for a different purpose. I shall treat public money as political money, since it is spent on the basis of political decisions. And I shall compare it with private money, with this end in view: to inquire into the fiscal behavior that public money induces and its relevance to the deficit.

My general hypothesis is this: The very publicness of public money opens the way for skilled professional politicians to barter it away to the best political advantage and thus contribute to the rising debt. Private money also invites skilled traders to barter it for economic advantage, but a comparison of the two as mediums of exchange will show that public money is the easier to manipulate to personal advantage. The points of comparison discussed are mode of acquisition, nature of ownership, method of distribution, incentives for saving, types of gratification, and program accounting.

Mode of Acquisition

Most working citizens, whether employers, employees, or private professionals, acquire money by exchanging one thing for another. Employers give wages or salaries in exchange for service; employees give service in exchange for money. Professionals provide services for a fee. Entrepreneurs develop products for a profit. So commonplace is this mode of acquiring money that the behavioral lesson it teaches goes practically unnoticed. Yet it is this lesson that makes for a healthy economy. It is this: Mutual satisfaction is the key to good economic exchange — to get money you have to give, and in fair measure. The wage or salary must be commensurate with the kind of labor expected, the labor rendered worthy of the pay, and the product worth the price. And unless both parties recognize this need for equity, economic exchange breaks down. Somebody suffers.

Wherein does this norm of fairness arise in economic transactions? What is its source? Many factors no doubt contribute to it, like personal standards of ethical conduct, cultural norms, and religious values. But this additional possibility should not be overlooked: *The very need for mutual satisfaction in order to acquire money in itself encourages fairness in economic transactions.* The point is simply this: How money is acquired molds the behavior of those acquiring it. He who labors under the necessity to give in order to get is already conditioned to be sensitive to the other party's self-interest in pursuit of his own.

Consider now the mode by which public money is acquired by members of Congress and the behavior that mode induces. They get it coercively, through taxing and borrowing, not voluntary exchange. The behavioral inferences are marked. At once the human element is removed, replaced by an automatic process. The exchange partner is no longer a person, a real human being. It is, instead, a faceless mass of taxpayers. Subtly the need for mutual satisfaction is eroded away, replaced by another type of need: to spend this money to the best political advantage.

What kind of fiscal behavior does this add up to? A sense of the matter may be gained through a hypothetical illustration. Imagine, if indeed one can, a voluntary tax system, one in which members of Congress could no longer get public money automatically by coercive taxation. Instead, in their capacity as purveyors of government goods and services, they would personally have to convince citizens of the need for these goods and services. Further, that the price was right. If citizens were not convinced, they could simply walk away, as they do in the marketplace. No deal.

What would be the behavioral effect on members of Congress? Would they be more sensitive to the need for mutual satisfaction in public expenditures? More cost-benefit-conscious? More in tune with the fiscal thinking of constituents? For them not to be would go against human nature itself.

Clearly the coercive mode for acquiring public money has significant behavioral implications for the way Congress spends. Getting money by fiat destroys the need for mutual satisfaction and opens the door for bartering money away to the best political advantage.

Nature of Ownership

The impact of ownership upon human behavior is everywhere evident. People who own their own homes are more apt to keep them up than are tenants. Farmers who work their own land are more likely than renters to follow practices designed to assure future fertility. Owners of businesses feel more personally responsible than even their best employees. Ownership is more than a legal claim: It constitutes the best prescription for caring behavior.

Private money is owned by citizens, and in most instances they show an owner's care in managing it. But as indicated, members of Congress only lay claim to somebody else's money. In behavioral terms, what difference does that make? To illustrate, consider yet another hypothetical illustration. When citizens pay taxes now they lose all track of their dollars; they have no idea how they are spent. But suppose that citizens could track their own tax money to its ultimate use as directed by Congress. In effect, they could make up their own minds about how well their dollars were spent.

What would be the likely behavioral impact on members of Congress? The point seems clear: Not only does how money is acquired make a difference; the nature of ownership also makes a big difference. The private ownership of money makes for care in its management, but the usership of someone else's money cuts that personal bond.

Method of Distribution

Mainly economic considerations direct the distribution of private dollars, while political considerations channel the flow of public dollars. How does the method of distribution affect fiscal behavior?

Economic considerations make for tightness in the distribution of dollars, but political considerations make for looseness. Consider why. Economic money, as Coleman pointed out, has a standard value that is quite uniform from place to place. Exchange rates may fluctuate, depending upon market conditions, but economic money as a medium of exchange tends to remain constant. As a result, the value of what is exchanged is always measured against a uniform monetary yardstick. And it is this uniform yardstick that makes for the tightness of economic exchange, because it narrows the opportunities for human manipulation.

Public money, however, having no standardized measure of worth, invites looseness in fiscal affairs. How much is a single vote worth? A thousand? A million? A political endorsement of a powerful organization?

A hefty Political Action Committee (PAC) contribution? Who knows? No one except the incumbent, who barters public money in exchange for political support.

Another factor making for looseness in the distribution of public money is that it cannot be monitored by the private citizens. In the retail marketplace consumers can protect themselves by comparison shopping. Should a product prove faulty, they can usually return it or have it fixed. But fiscal transactions in Congress are largely hidden from public scrutiny, so the members are free to exact as much political advantage as they can, unfettered by prying citizens. And since borrowing expands the supply of public money, the members can spend as much as it takes to achieve their desired political results.

The final reason the political distribution of public money makes for fiscal looseness rests in the nature of political competition. Businessmen competing in a free market must keep costs down because of competition. Competition in the political marketplace, however, works just the reverse, and for two reasons: logrolling and preemptive spending. In order for members of Congress to get what they want, they must go along with what all the others want, and spending thus escalates. And every incumbent engages in preemptive spending to discourage potential political challengers back home from entering the race against them. Overkill, fiscally speaking, is the result. Cost efficiency, it is clear, is not what counts in the distribution of public money, only political efficiency.

In sum, private money makes for tightness in management and public money for looseness because of fundamental differences governing their distribution. With its uniform monitory standards private money narrows the range for manipulation and barter. But without such standards public money widens that range. While economic exchanges involving private money can be monitored by both buyers and sellers, citizens are effectively isolated from political exchanges involving public money. And while economic competition tends to keep costs down, political competition drives them up.

Incentives for Saving

One of the most important properties of money, private or public, is that it can be saved. It represents a store of value that can be kept and spent later, when needed. That property in itself is great incentive for saving, and it tends to work that way in the private sector.

It does not, however, work that way in the public sector. Political rewards are reaped *only in spending*; if not spent, money's political value is quickly lost. The psychological message it sends is therefore clear: Spend; don't save. Further, if one member of Congress does not lay claim to his or her share, and quickly, another will. Thus while private money has its own built-in incentives for saving, public money is not only devoid of them; its incentives run in exactly the opposite direction.

Types of Gratification

The incentive to save private money, and spend public, defines the types of gratifications the two provide. When private money is saved it is usually with some long-term gratification in mind, like a college education for your children, a major purchase, investment, or retirement. The saver gives up consumption now in order to have something later. Such behavior is the stuff of wealth creation and economic development. It is, of course, not without risks. Money saved and invested may be lost. Investment outcomes are never certain, and examples of failures abound. Without saving, however, the economy stagnates. In a very real sense the economy depends on those who are willing to risk and wait.

But members of Congress, as I said, cannot wait for their political gratifications. And that is what makes borrowing for them so attractive. Its gratifications are immediate, its political risks few. Easy money, easy votes, almost certain reelection. That is the winning electoral formula.

What are the larger economic implications of this inherent conflict in gratifications between public and private money? They are, to say the least, far-reaching. Members of Congress will inevitably direct public money toward programs and projects that hold the prospect of quick, short-term payoffs. Their political interests are ill served by long-term public investments whose returns may be realized years later, after they have left office. When this happens, public money becomes the enemy of economic development, rather than the stimulator of it.

Program Accounting

The type of accounting I have in mind here is not concerned with how money is spent, but how well.

Observation suggests that private money spent for programs and projects, whether adding a new room to a home or a new plant to a manufacturing business, comes under reasonably strict scrutiny and simply because it is personally or corporately owned. So there is in the private sector a natural push to make sure that "we're getting our money's worth."

This is not the case with new government projects and programs. As indicated above, political rewards come in the spending, not in getting one's money's worth. If, perchance, it becomes known later that a program or project failed, there is no penalty. The political credit had been collected long since.

Imagine, however, another scenario. Suppose that under the principle of citizens' right to know, members of Congress were required to send every constituent an annual outsider, independent program audit for every program or project he or she ever voted for. Would the members of Congress then be more, or less, interested in making sure about getting their money's worthy? The human tendencies seem clear. Citizens would be more likely to demand better government and members of Congress to give it.

Table 1 summarizes the fiscal behaviors encouraged by private and public money.

TABLE 1
Private and Public Money, Their Related Fiscal Behaviors Compared

Variables	Private Money	Public Money
Method of Acquisition	Encourages mutual satisfaction in economic exchange.	Encourages bartering for political advantage.
Nature of Ownership	Makes for fiscal concern and caring.	Diminishes need for fiscal concern and caring.
Method of Distribution	Encourages tightness of control over spending.	Encourages looseness of control over spending.
Types of Gratification	Long-term gratification encourages saving.	Short-term gratification encourages spending.
Program Accounting	High demand for cost-effective programs and projects.	Low demand for cost-effective programs and projects.

CONCLUSION

That money and behavior are intimately related is an everyday observation. Too little suggests one kind of behavior, too much another. The poor behave one way, the rich in quite a different fashion. Indeed, money and the pursuit of it might be regarded as one of the most powerful shapers of human behavior.

But that public money, because it is political, may influence fiscal behavior quite differently than private money is a matter that has received less attention. This brief essay is only suggestive of the productive results that might accrue from a more systematic inquiry into the behavioral properties of public money.

This much can be said, however, on the basis of this brief foray into the subject: Citizens who expect Congress to manage the public purse with the same care they do their own are doomed to disappointment. It goes against human nature. The two purses send entirely different behavioral messages. And the better that is understood, the better the deficit will be understood.

Essay six, which follows, picks up on an idea just discussed. Earning money in the private economy, I suggested, encourages a recognition of the need for mutual satisfaction in both parties to the exchange. Now I shall consider the whole debt as an exchange between Congress and citizens to see what new insights that inquiry may yield.

6 Constituents and Congress: An Exchange View of the Debt

> Once one recognizes the ways in which human activity and choice depend upon rewards and punishments and the ways men reward and punish each other, one sees the basis of the conditioning of men by each other, and, more particularly, the basis for exchanging rewards and punishments as they try to motivate and affect each other.
> — Sidney R. Waldman

To this point members of Congress and their motives for deficit spending have been the focus. That focus is retained in this essay, but the frame is enlarged to include the Most Significant Others, citizens. Since it is citizens who both benefit from borrowed dollars and must repay them in one form or another, I shall regard the deficit as an exchange between the governors and the governed in which something is given, something taken back. This view will, I believe, add yet another perspective on the determining role of human nature in the deficit. It explains, in terms of the theory of social exchange, who has gotten the better of it, who the worst, how, and why.

EXCHANGE IN HUMAN AFFAIRS

The most common human activities are sometimes the most overlooked in terms of their larger social significance. Exchanges between and among people may be one of those. Without exchanges — whether they involve love and affection, cooperation, conflict, ideas, skills, goods, services, money, or just plain talk — there would be no families, no society, no institutions, no culture or civilization. We are an exchanging people and are the better for it. Long ago Adam Smith pronounced that trait to be the very basis of the economy when he spoke of our inherent tendency to "truck and barter" one thing for another. He might as well have been speaking for every other sphere of human activity, too.

Exchange, of course, is what representative government is about. From the smallest village council in the most remote area to Congress and the presidency, something of great value, the vote, is given in exchange for something of great worth, representation. And the subjects of exchange are as numerous as the joint concerns of citizens and government, education, health, safety, Social Security, banking, business, labor, commerce and trade, transportation, taxes, the environment, parks and public lands, national defense, foreign policy, food and agriculture, and on and on. The modes of political exchange are various, too, ranging in character from a franked congressional newsletter in a rural mailbox and, perchance, a penciled response scrawled at a kitchen table, to service club luncheons where local congressmen and congresswomen are featured speakers, to door-to-door campaign pitches, to candidates' tours through the local mall, to Political Action Committee (PAC) contributions and multi-million-dollar government contracts negotiated with the aid of an influential senator.

AN EXCHANGE TURNED SOUR

Then there is one of the longest-running political exchanges in modern history, the one over the debt. That it has turned sour is common knowledge, but if one wishes to document how sour, two sources of information do it well. The first are the public opinion polls for the last half-century, roughly the life span of the current debt. From them a singular pattern emerges, consistent and clear: As the debt rose, so did rank and file public resistance to it. It is just that simple.

Moreover, the members of Congress, who make opinion their business, were well aware of that. And how they responded is abundantly revealed in the other source, the *Congressional Record,* that unintended sourcebook on the political psychology of Congress and, in my view, one of the best. Read as history, the *CR* is a dull mishmash of speeches, resolutions, proceedings, and political trivia. But read as political psychology, the *Congressional Record* is an exciting and revealing look inside the political mind. And the speeches especially provide that look. They become not statements about issues of the day, but about two quite different things: the members' assessments of what their constituents thought about the issues of the day and their political response to it. Put another way, these speeches mirror both public opinion and the efforts of members of Congress to turn it to their political advantage.

How did they do that in the case of the debt? With some quite remarkable behavioral doublespeak: The more they raised the debt, the more speeches they made protesting it. In the early decades, when citizen opposition had not yet become organized and vocal, few members of Congress raised their voices against the debt. But as the debt grew, so did the speeches against it multiply, until, in 1985, when the Gramm-Rudman Act to eliminate the deficit by 1991 was in heated debate, the outpouring of rhetoric against the evils of debt filled most every page of the *Congressional Record*. Then even the staunch foes of Gramm-Rudman sang rhetorical hymns to fiscal prudence and balanced budgets.

Here are some random excerpts from the *CR* that tell the behavioral story.

So what do you want, my fellow Americans: a huge deficit that looms like a cloud on the horizon portending a dim future for your children and grandchildren, or do you wish to come to grips with the Federal budget, the same as we are required to come to grips with our own personal finances and the way we have to manage our own business affairs.

Letters, mailgrams and phone calls from interest groups are pouring in. The media has weighed in with a hand-wringing editorial campaign against its enactment. There is just one group that remains to be heard from: The American People. They know we're spending too much. They know we have demonstrated an uncontrollable urge to spend even more, and they want something done to stop it.

The time that we have discussed this issue has gone on for well over 20 years. It is not a new topic of the deficit. . . . But it's interesting for me to watch the accumulated vote of a variety of members of this Congress, where I find they consistently vote for programs that they know will spend us into deficit while at the same time they talk so openly and cry so loudly about the deficit and the accumulated debt at hand.

The big driving force behind the bill is that you can go tell the people that you voted for a balanced budget.

We know what has to be done — to limit defense spending, to limit entitlements, to raise revenue. But we refuse to move. No bill is going to replace the courage, the guts, and the leadership it takes to get action.

It would be hard to find in American fiscal history, I believe, another instance in which Congress was so successful over so many years, and in a matter touching the lives of so many, in pursuing a course of action so contrary to known popular public opinion.

In proposing to explain this mystifying political behavior in terms of the psychology of human exchange, I shall stay with the basic assumption that runs like a strong thread through all these essays: The reason for it has little or nothing to do with fiscal policy, but a great deal to do with the human nature of those who make fiscal policy. As proof of that consider this: In the 50 years of the deficit buildup one searches the *Congressional Record* in vain for a single defense of the deficit financing as good fiscal policy. There are speeches aplenty arguing for new expenditures or defending the old, both of which had the effect of continuously pushing the deficit up. But not one member of Congress during this time defended the fiscal result as desirable, only the actions creating it. One can only conclude that while deficit financing was being made the de facto fiscal policy of the land it was supported and sustained by an entirely invisible force: the desires of the political heart.

THE THEORY OF SOCIAL EXCHANGE

To my knowledge there is no single psychological theory that can fully explain what went wrong in the political exchange between Congress and citizens over the debt, how, or why. There is one, however, that adapts itself to that purpose, and admirably well. It is the theory of social exchange, the one Sidney Waldman used in his study of the foundations of political action, an excerpt from which appears at the beginning of this essay.[1]

Social exchange theory postulates that human interactions are best understood within the context of rewards and punishments. As Waldman stated, "Human activity and choice depend upon rewards and punishments" and it is through them that individuals "try to motivate and affect each other."[2] Rewards and punishments may be as fleeting as a smile or a frown, as determined as an "I will" or "I won't," as consequential as a pay raise or a dismissal, or as global as peace and war. But whatever their nature, they are the "basis of the conditioning of men by each other."

Two academic disciplines inform the concept of social exchange: learning psychology and economic theory. From learning psychology are drawn the concepts of rewards and punishments. The hypothesis is that rewards encourage desired learning and punishments discourage undesired learning. The psychological notion of reinforcement is also involved. Repeated rewards reinforce desired learning and improve the chances that the desired behavior will continue. Repeated punishments, or negative reinforcement, also aid desired learning by directing behavior away from undesired learning.

From economic theory are drawn the concepts of costs and benefits. Economic exchanges flourish when the benefits exceed the cost and cease when it is the other way around. Reinforcement is a relevant concept in economic exchange, too. Repeated benefits reinforce such exchanges and make more likely their repetition. And the threat of loss (another form of cost) should the exchange be discontinued tends toward the same result.

In sum, the theory of social exchange postulates the conditions governing human interactions. They are powered by the prospect of rewards and benefits and the threat of costs and punishments should they cease. Those exchanges that mutually reward and benefit, and repeatedly so, are likely to endure. By contrast, those in which the costs repeatedly outweigh the benefits, and thus punish, are likely to fall apart.

THE PSYCHOLOGY OF HUMAN EXCHANGES: SIX PROPOSITIONS

The following propositions seek to explain the rise and fall of human exchanges in terms of rewards and benefits, costs and punishments, and positive and negative reinforcement.[3]

Proposition One: Human exchanges are initiated in the prospect of mutual rewards and benefits.

Proposition Two: Human exchanges are repeated when reinforced positively by mutual rewards and benefits and negatively by the threat of costs and punishments should they cease.

Proposition Three: Too frequent reinforcements, however, lead to satiation, with both rewards and benefits and costs and punishments losing their power to influence behavior.

Proposition Four: Exchanges fall apart when one partner or both perceive that the costs and punishments exceed the rewards and benefits.

Proposition Five: Should one partner's costs and punishments, but not the other's, exceed his or her rewards and benefits, the other partner will persist in reaping the rewards and benefits, given the power to do so.

Proposition Six: Should that be the case, the disadvantaged partner will, given the power, fight back or withdraw from the exchange.

Consider briefly some of the wider implications of these propositions.

Proposition one asserts that limiting condition without which no voluntary human exchange can exist: mutual satisfaction. It is the glue of human exchange, whatever its nature. Without mutual satisfaction, exchanges are not likely to begin; without it, they cannot survive for long. Neither partner can have it entirely his own way: To get, he must give. In short, "good" human exchanges place constraints on human nature.

In considering political exchanges, another element must be reckoned with also. Private exchanges in a free society are voluntary, being constantly formed, cut off, and re-formed, depending upon how well they serve the mutual interests of the partners. Exchanges between Congress and citizens, however, are nonvoluntary, because the state by definition holds a monopoly on coercive power. In investigating the exchange over the deficit, then, we must determine what forms of state power enter into it, how they are employed, and with what behavioral results.

Proposition two asserts that condition that determines whether or not exchanges will be repeated: reinforcement. Reinforcement takes place, as indicated before, when each party receives a continuing flow of rewards and benefits, coupled with a threat of costs and punishments should the desired behavior cease. When that behavior continues, each party will flourish and prosper.

Proposition two, however, does not define mutual rewards and benefits as necessarily equal. Parity may be critical to those economic exchanges in which the partners' financial investments are identical. But in most exchanges it is sufficient that each partner see his or her own rewards and benefits as exceeding the costs and punishments. That is an adequate condition for achieving reinforcement and permitting the exchange to be repeated.

There is still another factor that bears significantly on proposition two, determining the way in which exchanges will be repeated. It is the amount of reinforcement each partner receives. Large rewards and benefits, coupled with the threat of large costs and punishments should the exchange cease, make for a strong desire to see it repeated. Small rewards and benefits, on the other hand, coupled with the prospect of only small costs and punishments should it cease, make for an indifferent commitment to its repetition. The implications of this condition for political exchanges between members of Congress and citizens seem clear. One needs to inquire into the degree of advantage each sees in the arrangement. The greater the advantage a partner perceives, the more likely he or she will persist in it. Contrarily, the less advantage, the less likely he or she will back it strongly. Should this be the case, the exchange may continue under the strong auspices of one partner, but with only the acquiescence of the other.

Proposition three takes into account the reality of reinforcement overload. Too frequent rewards and benefits and too numerous threats of costs and punishments diminish their power as agents of behavioral change. Proposition three does not predict, however, when satiation will set in; that depends upon the particular situation. It only suggests that at some point it can and, in that event, the stimulus value of repeated reinforcement falls sharply off.

One inference of proposition three for political exchanges is that governmental rewards and benefits will be perceived as good only up to a point. What is regarded as "good" by citizens in the beginning may, after too many repetitions, come to be regarded with indifference or even as "bad."

Another implication is of a more profound sort. It has to do with the "fit" between the rewards and benefits offered by government and human needs and wants of the kind set forth by Maslow and discussed in essay four. The closer the fit, the less likely it is that satiation will set in, but the rougher the fit, the more likely. In other words, we tire more quickly of the things we do not like, but less quickly of those we do.

This view is very much in line with that of the political thinkers whose voices were recalled in essay two. They all began their formulations not with government, it will be recalled, but with propositions about human nature. Upon those they then erected their conceptions of what kind of government is best. The quest for more perfect government is inevitably a quest for a more perfect union of human nature and government.

Today our view of human nature is wider and more various than ever before. The more we learn about it, the more we marvel at its rich complexity. Human beings, we now recognize, are more than any single ideological conception of them. They are more than political, more than economic, more than worker, more than procreator, more than religious, and more than citizen. They are all of these multiplied a hundredfold. It follows, then, that government exchanges that allow for human catholicity will outlast those based on narrow political ideology alone. Any ideology that construes human beings too parochially simply will not fit their nature. In time, they will find a way to say so.

Deficit spending's ideological view of voters is as avid consumers of government goods and services. Is it possible that view is becoming dysfunctional and voters are saying they want more discretion over their own spending? That possibility should not be discounted.

Proposition four is the inverse of proposition two: Human exchanges flourish on positive and negative reinforcement but fall apart for the lack of them. Just as proposition three recognizes the reality of satiation, proposition four recognizes the reality of costs and punishments. There are no rewards and benefits in human exchange without costs and punishments. The former exist only as a favorable balance against the latter. When the balance is unfavorable, the exchange dissolves.

Proposition four has a number of implications for political exchanges. One is that in every exchange both the governors and the governed make running calculations about the balance of rewards and benefits as against costs and punishments. Each has a view in terms of his or her self-interests and will behave accordingly. Members of Congress will avoid those exchanges with constituents that are politically costly and punitive. On the other hand, they will aggressively promote those that are politically rewarding and beneficial. Citizens will do the same with respect to their own self-interests. They will favor those political exchanges that yield more rewards and benefits than costs and punishments and avoid those that do not.

Proposition five predicts what happens when one partner's costs and punishments, but not the other's, exceed his or her rewards and benefits. The partner with the advantage will, given the power, persist in the exchange. This proposition brings into sharp focus two hard realities: the great force of rewards and benefits in influencing human behavior and the determining role of external power. It says, in effect, that rewards and benefits, especially if they are substantial, will not be given up easily and will not be given up at all if the partner with the advantage has sufficient leverage over the other to keep them coming.

External power may take many forms — money, legal leverage, law, control over agendas, information, channels of communication, experience, monopoly, office, status, concentrations of resources, weight of numbers, and on and on. Whatever its form, however, overriding power in any human exchange has this effect: *It precludes mutual satisfaction and makes the disadvantaged partner's human needs and wants irrelevant, a mere instrument to the advantaged partner's ends.*

The implications of proposition five for political exchanges are disturbingly clear. If one suspects that overriding power is a deciding factor, he must inquire into its nature and exercise. Political power, I suspect, figures strongly in perpetuating our regime of debt. I shall therefore have to inquire into its nature and the modes by which it is exercised.

Another implication derives from proposition five that has to do with how a government achieves, maintains, and loses legitimacy with the citizenry. This proposition suggests that the balance of rewards and benefits between the two parties determines legitimacy. Governments achieve and maintain legitimacy when the balance favors citizens. They lose it when citizens perceive that the balance has tipped toward government. And if citizens perceive that, it already has.

The final proposition, six, asserts what the disadvantaged partner will do should his or her costs and punishments exceed the rewards and benefits. Given the power, he or she will fight back or withdraw from the exchange. Here too, the power factor is critical. Fighting back may be costly in terms of money, time, and energy, making it next to impossible.

In terms of political exchanges involving the state, the costs for most citizens of fighting back are out of reach. These costs are manageable only by those with huge resources of money and electoral power. And, even withdrawing voluntarily from the state is a near impossibility, short of actual migration. It may be for this reason that symbolic withdrawal from politics is so prevalent in the nation today, like not voting. It is common to attribute low voter turnout to lack of interest, education, or civic-mindedness. I am more inclined to think, however, that not voting may be better explained in terms of propositions five and six. Increasing numbers of people sense that in their exchanges with government the costs and punishments outweigh the rewards and benefits and costless symbolic withdrawal is their best way of protesting — in other words, an ordinary citizen's way of "getting back."

PROPOSITIONS APPLIED TO
THE DEFICIT EXCHANGE

Propositions one and two speak to the decades of the thirties and forties, the period of the Great Depression and World War II. In the depths of the depression there were no jobs; there was no money. Breadlines were long and daily growing longer. The seeds of discontent were being sown everywhere, and anarchy threatened. Deficit spending was not an option; it was a necessity. It held the only prospect for "priming the economic pump," "getting the jobless off the dole," and eliminating the only thing the nation had to fear, "fear itself," as President Roosevelt put it. Most people regarded borrowing as in everyone's mutual interest. Repeated borrowing reinforced the pattern, since it seemed to ease, but certainly did not cure, the depression.

World War II came hard on the heels of the depression and continued into the mid-forties. The pattern of deficit financing continued, and with broad popular support. Hitler had to be defeated and the Japanese war machine smashed. That took borrowed money, lots of it. But the need to borrow was never questioned. In fact, citizens made it a point of pride to be the lenders by regularly purchasing government war bonds.

In retrospect, it was those years of depression and war that defined citizens' tolerance for national debt. It was a time of clear national crisis. In this regard citizens were only listening to their own fiscal history.

Earlier Congresses had always operated on the assumption that balanced budgets were a part of an "unwritten fiscal constitution." Thomas Jefferson had set the tone. "Public debt," he said, "is one of the greatest dangers to be feared by Republican governments."[4] Alexander Hamilton, who perhaps more than anyone else shaped our early fiscal policy, counseled that "in view of the perpetual tendency to the accumulation of debt there ought to be perpetual, anxious, and increasing effort to reduce that which at any time exists." James Madison vowed that one of the primary goals of his administration was "to liberate the public resources by an honorable discharge of public debts." And John Quincy Adams found a balanced budget to be a sound maxim for the political economy. "Stewards of the public money," he declared, "should always keep expenditures of the year within the limits of receipts."

Among the nation's early political leaders, the argument against debt had a distinctly populist ring: Debt was harmful to the working classes. Interest payments on it represented a redistribution of income from the lower to the upper classes, since only the latter could afford to buy government bonds. "Interest," Andrew Jackson's secretary of the treasury pointed out, "is now paid to capitalists out of the profits of labor." Were that not necessary, labor would be "released from this burden, but capital, thus thrown out of productive use, will seek a productive employment, giving thereby a new impetus to enterprise in agriculture, the arts, commerce and navigation."

And these early leaders practiced fiscally what they preached. The Revolutionary War debt of $80 million was cut in half by 1811. The War of 1812 tripled the debt, but by the 1830s it had been almost eliminated. It rose again during the Mexican War but then decreased until the Civil War. The War between the States really put the "unwritten fiscal constitution" to the test. It produced a $2.8 billion national debt, the highest ever. But Congress again responded positively. It centralized spending by creating two powerful appropriation committees, each of which rode hard on new spending requests. In 31 years, 1867–97, not only was the Civil

War debt paid off; there were 27 surpluses. And in 13 of those 27 years revenues exceeded expenditures by more than 25 percent.

The 1896 recession combined with the Spanish-American War to initiate 20 years with 11 debts, but by the time the United States entered World War I the debt was back down to what it had been in 1896. During World War I, the debt increased twentyfold, to $25.8 billion. But again Congress tightened its spending and shrank the debt to $16 billion. And that is where it stood when the stock market crashed in 1929, setting the stage for the depression of the thirties.

The fifties came. The Great Depression was over, and World War II had been won. The nation was shifting back reasonably well to a peace-time economy. There were ups and downs, but the economic indicators were generally up. According to historic precedent, it was time for Congress to start paying off in this period of relative prosperity that which had been borrowed in war and depression. Then the unprecedented happened: Congress went right on borrowing as before, except for other purposes. This time Congress borrowed not for national purposes in which citizens could take mutual satisfaction, but to attract new political constituencies with particularized benefits, such as entitlements, subsidies, and tax breaks and preferences. Deficit spending in the space of one decade was thoroughly politicized. Never again would there be a national consensus regarding the need for it.

Another aspect of proposition two was illustrated during the fifties. It postulates, it will be recalled, that the relative amounts of rewards and benefits each partner receives, coupled with the size of the costs or punishments should the exchange cease, determine the strength of their commitments to it. As for citizens, it was not yet clear in the fifties how continued borrowing would affect their personal futures. Not until the accumulated effects of the debt began to be felt in the seventies would that become painfully evident. But for members of Congress the political dividends of deficit spending were immediate. Constituencies expanded wonderfully in response to receiving those particularized benefits, making reelection almost a certainty. In street language, the members had become "hooked" on debt, and to risk the perils of political life without them had become unthinkable. Addiction was close at hand.

Signs of citizen satiation, proposition three, began to appear in the sixties. To the war in Vietnam was added the War on Poverty. Fiscal fatigue was setting in. Serious questions began to be raised about whether the nation could afford both "guns and butter." A phrase that had been around for a while now gained wide currency: "throwing money at problems." It summed up the increasing disenchantment of citizens with the steadily rising deficit.

But it was not until the seventies that, for most citizens, the accumulated costs and punishments of the mounting debt really began to strike home. It was the decade of proposition four: The cost and punishments were definitely outweighing the rewards and benefits. Double digit inflation, double digit interest rates, and rising unemployment were connected in the public mind with the rising deficit. It now became clear to most citizens that the debt was a losing proposition.

The time of proposition five was at hand. One partner was clearly disadvantaged. What would the other do? Congress acted as predicted: It went right on borrowing, pausing only long enough to make, in Gramm-Rudman, a cynical symbolic gesture toward a balanced budget. Gramm-Rudman, it can now be seen, was to law what all those speeches opposing the deficit were to rhetoric: behavioral doublespeak. In the years since Gramm-Rudman's passage, its annual deficit targets have never been met except by juggling the government's books. In real dollars, the debt continues to rise as it did before the measure was passed. In effect, nothing has changed.

And that brings us to the current era, postulated in proposition six. Current public opinion polls suggest that citizens are now cynical, too. They don't expect Congress to change its fiscal spots. Some still fight bravely on against the deficit, but most seem simply to have given up. "A curse on both your Houses," as it were.

One is tempted to conclude that the least damage of the debt is fiscal; we can, likely will, survive that. The real wound, and one that will be harder to survive, is that inflicted by Congress via the debt on representative democracy. That infliction could be more permanent than we have permitted ourselves to think about. In time we may come to think of it that way. Some years from now we will see that, if I may be permitted to repeat myself, the argument about the debt was not about money at all; it was about the way perpetual deficit spending caused us to be governed when we really deserved much better from those with whom we had entered into a political exchange.

SUMMARY

The contribution of social exchange theory to an understanding of human relations rests in this: It makes clear the need for two essentials notably lacking in the exchange between Congress and citizens over the deficit — mutual satisfaction and equal power. Without those, human exchanges fall apart.

Is there in the real world a model of exchange that incorporates these two requirements? There is, and it is one with which most citizens are totally familiar: the marketplace.[5] Here the customer in pursuit of the best buy meets the economists' economic man in pursuit of a profit. Self-interest pitted face to face with self-interest. Yet somehow, these directly competing interests get resolved, and in most cases with mutual satisfaction. Why and how?

The answer will be found in two concepts embedded in the theory of markets but totally absent from the theory of politics. They are perfect and imperfect competition. Perfect competition is an ideal and as such is seldom seen in pure form in any marketplace. But it is approached when buyer and seller meet with equal power. With money equal to that of the price, the buyer is free to buy, or not, as he or she chooses. In turn, the seller's power resides in the product, whose value we shall presume is worth the price. Thus is laid the basis for mutual satisfaction in exchange: One party wants the product, the other the money. In swapping, something spontaneous happens: *Each serves the self-interest of the other*. But note that it does so only by placing limits on the power of each partner. Neither party can have both the product and the money. To get, each must give, and equally.

Now note the absence of such restrictions in imperfect competition, in which one party holds some power advantage over the other, making mutual satisfaction impossible. Perhaps the seller must sell or the buyer must buy. The seller may know the fine print, the buyer not. The seller may have a monopoly and thus be able to extract an unreasonably high price. Or the seller may have market information affecting the price of which the seller is unaware. But whatever the nature of the power advantage, it makes achieving mutual satisfaction remote, if not impossible.

Another way to put the concepts of perfect and imperfect competition is in terms of game theory. When both partners win, and equally so, the result is described as a "positive sum game." It is perfectly fair. But when one partner has some type of power advantage over the other, the result is a zero sum game, because his gain represents the loss of the other. It is imperfect.

We come now to the critical question to which this summary inevitably leads: Should political exchanges be bound by the codes of the marketplace? Should the concept of perfect competition be used to measure them?

That question places my central thesis about human nature and the deficit squarely to the test. If one thinks of government as a disembodied institution, deriving its powers somehow from extrahuman considerations like ideology or "what is best for people," the concept of human exchange and the need for limitations like mutual advantage and equal power is pure nonsense. But if one begins his thinking with human nature as the common denominator of both the governed and the governors, it is the only code that makes sense. Otherwise, we have precisely what we see in the debt, an expression of imperfect competition in which the gain of one is the loss of the other.

III RED INK AND REPRESENTATIVE DEMOCRACY

7 Democracy in Debt: Paradox or Pathology?

> There was a man in the land of Uz, whose name
> was Job; and that man was blameless and upright.
> — Job 1:1

The Old Testament story of Job is well known, as is the moral paradox it poses.[1] Though a good man, and just, Job was nevertheless beset by evil. The Sabeans fell upon his oxen and asses in the fields, slew the servants tending them, and drove the animals away. The Chaldeans made a similar raid on his camels. While his sons and daughters were feasting in a brother's house a great wind sprang up and blew it in, killing them all. Finally, after a succession of other tragedies, ugly sores disfigured and tortured him. Through the rich imagery of the King James Bible the reader can almost see Job sitting there, reduced now to sackcloth and ashes, pondering the eternal paradox of why good is beset by evil.

In this essay I ponder this: Why is representative democracy, so seemingly good, beset by a debt so demonstrably bad?

Job, in his search for an answer, had a recourse we do not. He could say, and did, that the answer lay not in himself, but in the mysterious ways of God. We, however, cannot excuse ourselves so easily, for the debt has representative government stamped all over it. It was not imposed on us from the outside. Nor is it the result of some centralized regime's bungled economic planning. The men and women we sent to Congress through free and open elections created it. There can be little doubt: In terms of the process that produced it, the debt is democratically ours.

Yet who would claim that it also represents the will of the people? The debt is decried on every side for the billions it soaks up in interest payments when the money is sorely needed elsewhere, for the way it drives up interest rates and inflation, and for the way it mortgages everyone's future, even that of the unborn. How can one explain how a seemingly good system of governance is capable of producing such fiscal evil?

The viewpoint presented here is that the classical view of democracy, the one many of us learned in high-school civics, did not prepare us for the realities of democratic practice. Drawing its inspiration from democracy's ideology, it sees the debt only as a paradox, a contradiction that should not have happened. It can explain it only in terms of fiscal and moral backsliding.

There is another view of democracy, however, that can and does make sense of the debt. It takes its inspiration not from ideology, but from the realities of democratic politics. It sees democracy not as a disembodied set of ideals, but as a human process capable of both great good and great evil.

If one holds to this latter view, the debt takes on a very different meaning. It comes to be seen not as a paradox to wring hands over, but as an incipient pathology to guard against. In the discussion that follows I examine each of these views, then conclude with some observations about how they contribute to a better understanding of what needs to be done if the problem of the debt is to be solved.

THE CLASSICAL VIEW OF DEMOCRACY

Pure in its formulation, the classical view takes its inspiration, as just indicated, from democratic ideology. Defined as that arrangement by which people make political decisions through their elected representatives, it makes the people sovereign. And in their sovereignty they actually *make* the government. In this, their role is similar to that of active stockholders in the affairs of a company. They elect members of Congress as stockholders might elect members of the board. They take a lively interest in government, as stockholders would in the company's affairs. They formulate well thought out positions on current issues. And they convey them regularly to their elected representatives, as stockholders would to company directors.

In the classical view, citizens are high-minded. Generous, they never use government to gain advantage over others. Rational, they always let logic, not personal interest, guide their public decisions.

Such idealized citizens are the spiritual descendants of Rousseau's "noble savage," primitive man uncontaminated by civilization. "He breathes only peace and liberty," the French philosopher wrote of this man. "Innocent of pride and greed, he was driven only by his passion for generosity and friendship." After he had dined, Rousseau went on: "He is at peace with all nature and is a friend to all his fellow creatures." In short, he was naturally good.

Representatives of the people, in the classical view, share the nobility of Rousseau's primitive man. Devoid of self-interests, they seek only the common good. Like the citizens who elect them, they are rational; reason, not passion, guides their legislative and political behavior. As legislators, they act as instructed delegates of the voters. Ever obedient to the voters' wishes, they work to incorporate these desires into appropriate laws, policies, and programs. Their motives for being in politics spring from the desire to serve, and upon attaining office they feel sworn to make their constituents' interests, not their own, paramount.

Government, in classical doctrine, has no will of its own. Having none, it cannot be at variance with the people's will. What is government, then? It is the repository of the people's will, holding it in trust until elected representatives act. As an institution, government is a handmaiden of the people, nothing more, nothing less. Being the instrument of their will, it is ever sensitive to their wishes and wants and, of course, innocent of evil.

In view of this ideological orientation it is not surprising, then, that the classical conception of democracy can explain the debt only as something that should not have happened and likely would not had Congress only practiced some old-time fiscal religion. The solution, then, is straightforward: Persuade Congress to stop its backsliding ways and return to the straight and narrow budgetary path. In other words, the answer rests in remaking human nature, convincing it to be good, instead of bad.

But the convincing, we know, has failed, because the diagnosis is wrong. If citizens and representatives were as high-minded as the classical doctrine assumes them to be and the government as benign, a debt so large as to threaten nearly everyone's economic well-being would be unthinkable. Obviously, we need to reconsider our view of what democracy is really about. Then the debt will come to be seen not as a paradox, but as a deeply rooted pathology for which appropriate measures should be taken.

DEMOCRACY DEFINED AS THE COMPETITIVE STRUGGLE FOR VOTES

This other view of democracy takes its cue, as was said previously, not from ideology, but from political practice. Joseph Schumpeter captured this view in his study of *Capitalism, Socialism, and Democracy,* where he defined democracy as "the institutional arrangement for arriving at political decisions in which individuals (candidates) acquire the power to decide by means of a competitive struggle for the people's vote."[2] The key words are "power," "competitive struggle," and "vote." To put Schumpeter's definition in the vernacular, democracy comes out as the bloody struggle among politicians for people's votes in order to achieve and hold political power.

While the classical view comes close to denying human nature a role in the affairs of government, Schumpeter's definition places it squarely at the center. It makes no pretense that a legislative body is like a collection of instructed delegates seeking only to do the people's will. It rejects the implication that election to high office turns men and women suddenly angelic. It assumes that politicians, with their strong urges to power, will themselves make the government the sovereignty of the people, limited to voting politicians into, or out of, office.

After redefining democracy in terms of the competitive struggle for the people's vote, Schumpeter proceeded to spell out how this view helps to explain certain realities of democratic politics and certain democratic pathologies. The following discussion draws its inspiration from Schumpeter's thinking on these two matters, but I have added collaborative evidence from two other observers: James McGregor Burns and Anthony Downs.

REALITIES OF DEMOCRATIC POLITICS

Three realities of democratic politics become more understandable, Schumpeter asserts, when democracy is defined as the competitive struggle for people's votes.[3] The first reality is that politicians dominate the democratic process, the second that Congress is a body of professional politicians, and the third that the sovereignty of citizens is quite rigidly proscribed.

The Dominance of Politicians

The view that democracy is the competitive struggle for votes automatically shifts the prime source of political energy from the people to politicians. Scattered, unorganized, and occupied with their daily rounds, the people of necessity stand at the margins of the political process. Democracy, in a very real sense, then, is government by elected politicians. They, not the people, actually make it.

This activist role of congressional politicians was well described by James McGregor Burns. "Congressmen do not wait for pressure from home," this longtime student of Congress observed. "They take the initiative, moving to protect interest groups before any pressure is in sight. As active propagandists they convert their offices into temporary headquarters for politically mobilized groups. They are, in fact, lobbyists, but they work at the core of government, rather than at its periphery. They are the makers of pressure, not merely the subjects of it."[4]

The conclusion is very clear: Members of Congress are not only guided by public opinion; to the extent they can, they dominate it, too.

Congress as a Body of Professional Politicians

The Founding Fathers would likely be shocked at the current composition of Congress. They anticipated that the national legislature would be a citizens' body composed of persons who left their private occupations for periods of time to serve government. The idea was to keep Congress close to the people by an ever renewed membership.

Current reality, of course, is very different. The constant competitive struggle for the people's votes hones incumbents' political skills to a sharp edge and helps to keep them in office. Further, incumbents, who command all the resources of office, are effective in using these resources to outcampaign challengers for their seats. The result is that Congress may be now quite properly described as a tenured body of elected bureaucrats.

The Proscribed Sovereignty of Citizens

As every small stockholder in a huge corporation knows, he or she "makes" the company in only a very limited sense. It is professional management that really makes the company and determines its destiny. The same may be said of individual voters in our large and complex democracy. Only in a most limited and general way do they influence government. Their role is restricted to electing those who do. The people's sovereignty, then, is always conditioned by this fact: Professional politicians are in charge, and the latitude they have in setting the public agenda, and making public choices, is both wide and far-reaching.

In sum, the three realities of democratic politics do not fit the classical view of democracy. But when viewed as consequences of the competitive struggle for votes they begin to make a great deal of sense. Notice, now, how the same may be said of democracy's pathologies.

DEMOCRATIC PATHOLOGIES

Like democratic practices, the pathologies of democracy become more understandable when seen as the consequence of the competitive struggle for the people's votes. Consider six such pathologies.

Expedient Politics

The competitive struggle for votes requires members of Congress constantly to bend politics to the needs of the moment. Always in a fight for their political lives, they are forever on trial. Bobbing and weaving is essential for survival; staying too long with an unpopular, though correct, principle only invites defeat. Thus competitive politics, by the nature of its survival requirements, is always adaptive, always opportunistic, always on the lookout for the main chance.

Short-term Views

Expedient politics inevitably makes for short-term views and solutions. Intent upon the current political scene, congressional incumbents have little or no time to think ahead or even to consider the long-term consequences of their daily actions. Citizens can always hope that those consequences are positive or, at least, benign. But there can be no guarantee of that. The final results may just as easily be disastrous.

Distorted Issues

In political warfare every issue must be treated not in terms of its inherent worth, but on the basis of its political merits or demerits. The careful weighing of pros and cons, the making of informed judgments, and waiting for all the evidence to come in must all be sacrificed to the requirements of the competitive political struggle. Each question, regardless of its merit, must always be given a political spin. This necessity gives added weight to the conception that politicians are perforce "dealers in votes." Issues are only means; votes are the end.

Unkept Campaign Promises

The common complaint that "candidates promise one thing but do another once in office" must also be viewed as a part of the competitive struggle for votes. The classical conception of democracy assumes that candidates seek office in order to help shape and influence policy. But a more realistic view suggests just the reverse: They shape proposal in order to win. Campaign come-ons, then, are in a very real sense incidental to the execution of office.

Politics is not the only place, of course, where incidental functions are used in the pursuit of private desires. As political scientist Anthony Downs points out in his insightful work on the economic theory of democracy: "Even in the real world almost nobody carries out his function ... purely for its own sake. Rather, such function is discharged by someone who is spurred to act by private motives logically irrelevant to his function. Thus, social functions are usually the by-product, and private ambitions the ends, of human action."[5]

Pressure Groups

Much current criticism of pressure groups centers on their unsavory influence on members of Congress. Such criticism ignores, however, the latent functions they serve, like helping incumbents in their competitive struggle for votes. In reality, the relationship between the members of Congress and pressure groups is symbiotic, mutually advantageous. Pressure groups provide incumbents with campaign money and votes; the latter reciprocate with influence and legislative favors. The two are in reality exchange partners seeking mutual gain.

Corruption

Just as economic corruption arises in the struggle for profit, political corruption springs from the competitive drive for votes. The cause in each has a common source: the urge to power.

To summarize, the pathologies of democracy arise in the competitive struggle for the people's votes. The struggle causes politics to be bent to the exigencies of the moment, public issues to be given a political spin, short-term views to prevail, pressure groups to thrive, and political corruption to exist. While these are explained by the classical view of democracy as moral lapses, democracy defined as the competitive struggle for votes regards them as lapses in our ability to curb and control human nature's undesirable effects on the body politic.

IMPLICATIONS FOR THE DEBT

If Schumpeter's view of democracy as a competitive struggle for the people's vote is correct, what does that imply about the debt as a democratic pathology? James Madison, it seems to me, gave the best generalized answer when he wrote: "In framing a government which is to be administered by men over men, the greatest difficulty lies in this: You must first enable the government to control the governed; and in the next place oblige it to control itself."[6] Realist about human nature that he was, Madison did not trust to moral persuasion to keep it in check. Should good government, he seems to have asked himself, depend upon convincing the people within it to be good? Or should the rules governing their conduct be so drawn as to protect against the bad, even in the best of them? Madison, we know, chose the latter. Refusing to make government hostage to human nature, he set about devising his checks and balances among the three branches. What he was checking, of course, was not government, but human nature in government. If he could do that, goodness, he figured, would at least have a chance to show its fair face.

At this point in time the deficit is hostage to human nature. We will have caught up with the wisdom of Madison when we fully realize that and insist that Congress develop similar checks and balances in the fiscal arena over which it presides.

When Job was beset by troubles, three old friends came to visit. As might be expected of old friends, they did more than commiserate: They each made a diagnosis of, and a prescription for, his afflictions. There were differences of opinion among them, but on two matters all three agreed. Job was obviously guilty of some great sin; otherwise he would not have been visited by such great evil. And he should forthwith repent of it. If he did that, God would forgive, Job's torments would vanish, and he would be restored to health and prosperity. But Job resisted both conclusions and continued to think of his afflictions as a paradox, something that should not happen to a good man under God's moral order.

And we can continue to wonder why the debt is inconsistent with democracy's assumed moral order. Or we can see it as entirely consistent with democracy's natural order and then set about developing rules that checkmate it in the interest of the common good.

8   Debt and the Democratic Order

> Our electoral process is flowing from the hands of
> the people to the pocketbooks of the few and a
> megabuck campaign.
>
> — Congressman Bruce Vento

This radical shift in electoral power away from the people, here lamented
by Congressman Vento of Minnesota,[1] is redefining representative
democracy in our time. "To represent" is coming to mean to cater to those
special interests who have the money and/or the electoral clout to keep
one in office. "To be represented" is coming to mean to have the money
and/or electoral influence to buy "access" to someone in office. Access,
once thought to be a democratic right, now carries a price. Those who
can pay it are economically advantaged through government. Those who
get it are politically advantaged in government. Meanwhile, the people are
disadvantaged by government.

How did we come to this perversion of our democratic order? One
hears a number of explanations, but one stands out. The high cost of
campaigning, it is said, forces members of Congress "to sell their
political souls" in exchange for campaign money. They would rather not,
but they have no choice. They must go where the "deep pockets" are.

Such an explanation, I believe, confuses cause with effect. It assumes
that the "pocketbooks of the few" and the "megabuck" campaigns they
make possible are the reasons "our electoral process is flowing from the
hands of the people." Ignored is this prior consideration: What opened
the floodgates in the first place for money to overwhelm the electoral
process? That is the real question, and the answer will be found, I
believe, in our 60-year regime of debt. It denied people fiscal control over
the public purse; the loss of electoral control to the "pocketbooks of the

few" and "megabuck" campaigns were but natural consequences, the spawning of our far deeper fiscal malaise. What is frequently forgotten is that federal borrowing is an undemocratic mode of government financing. In contrast to taxing, which inevitably arouses public debate, borrowing is a quiet affair discreetly engineered by Congress. All it involves is a vote to raise the debt ceiling, and new money to spend comes pouring into the Treasury. The people are effectively cut out of the process. In a very real sense, borrowing is of Congress, not the people.

In the introduction to this volume, it may be recalled, I suggested that taxing and borrowing are far more than two ways to finance the costs of government: They are distinctly different forms of government. Here we have graphic evidence of that. Only under a longtime regime of debt could Congress and special interest groups have become what I shall hereafter call the Alphas and Betas of political power or citizens have been reduced to the role of Significant Others, as I shall refer to them. Had the members been required to raise their constituents' taxes every time they wanted to bestow some new government entitlement, human nature being what it is, the chances are they would have thought twice. Only because they could quietly raise the debt ceiling, borrow unlimited amounts of money, and distribute it in politically strategic places did this shift in electoral power away from the people take place. The "pocketbooks of the few" and "megabuck" campaigns are not causes; they are but sorry effects, the price the polity pays for a regime of debt.

Another way of saying all this is that balanced and unbalanced budgets in a democratic order distribute power very differently. Schematically, the distributions are shown in Table 2.

Thus with balanced budgets citizens are the Alphas of electoral power, Congress the Betas, and special interests the Significant Others. But unbalanced budgets stand that power ranking on its head. Congress

TABLE 2
Distribution of Political Power, Balanced and Unbalanced Budgets

Power Ranking	Balanced Budgets	Unbalanced Budgets
Alphas, First in Power:	Citizens	Congress
Betas, Second in Power:	Congress	Special Interests
Significant Others, Last in Power:	Special Interests	Citizens

goes to top and citizens to the bottom, while special interests move in between.

A word now about the focus of this essay. Both sharp and specific, it is on one of the forces that facilitated this redistribution of power. I refer to our existing fiscal order. And by fiscal order I mean simply Congress's system for raising revenue and spending it. The question addressed, then, is this: What is there about the fiscal order that makes it easy to pervert the democratic order? The answer, I shall find, is in its natural spending bias. It is programmed in favor of the spenders and against the payers. The very way Congress goes about collecting and spending helps to explain why Congress and special interests have become the Alphas and Betas of electoral power. They first became the Alphas and Betas of fiscal power. It explains, too, why the people have been reduced to the status of Significant Others in electoral power. They were first stripped of their fiscal power.

In pursuit of this hypothesis I shall, in "The Advantaged Spenders," look at the spending side of the fiscal order for the way it empowers the Alphas and Betas. The key reason will be found in the way spending is concentrated on the few, but the costs are distributed among the many. Then, in "The Disadvantaged Payers," I shall focus on the revenue side. The several modes of raising revenue — taxing, borrowing, and money inflation — are examined for the way they disempower the payers. The focus will be on the fiscal illusions each mode evokes, making it almost impossible for the citizens to know whether they are getting their money's worth.

THE ADVANTAGED SPENDERS

Before examining the spending biases of the fiscal order, it will be useful to call to our aid two comparatively recent historical developments. They help to explain why the members of Congress have exploited so aggressively the advantages that the existing fiscal order affords them. I refer to the decline of political parties as shapers of candidates and party policy and to the erosion of central power within Congress as an institution. The combined effect of these was to cut the members off from important institutional support and policy guidance, making them, in effect, private political entrepreneurs, "dealers in votes," as Joseph Schumpeter described them. Like all entrepreneurs, they needed working capital, and they found it in deficit spending. It easily converted to campaign contributions and electoral support.

Some Historical Perspective

Once, not too many decades ago, political parties played a dominant role in selecting, "grooming," and supporting candidates for Congress. The help the old-line parties provided did not match that of parliamentary democracies, like Great Britain for example, but at least they relieved candidates of the necessity to play Santa Claus to every interest group in order to stay in office. The fiscal consequences of this historic change are well known: Incumbents now return from the campaign trail with stacks of political IOUs that somehow, someday, will have to be paid off.

The decentralization of congressional power paralleled the decline of party power.[2] In earlier decades the powers of Congress were tightly held in the hands of the Speaker and a small number of committees whose chairmen had long seniority. This was true, especially, of the committees having to do with money. Even more important was the way these powerful chairmen thought of their roles; they tended to regard themselves as watchdogs of the national treasury.

Now the old committee system has been shattered into over 200 pieces, if one counts all the standing, sub-, and special committees. Congress, even historically, never was a single, deliberative body, but now it is more like a collection of 535 political fiefdoms, each furiously bidding for public funds to sustain its own independent operations.

In citing these historic changes I do not intend to defend the old against the new; the changes were probably overdue. The old-line parties produced a lot of political hacks, and some of the old-line congressional leadership was autocratic in the extreme. I am simply noting how these changes created in the members of Congress new demands for political "working capital," which they found in deficit spending. They were motivated as never before to exploit every political advantage the system of financing government provides them.

Concentrated Benefits, Dispersed Costs

The greatest single advantage that the Alphas and Betas have as spenders is best explained by what some economists refer to as the "concentrated benefits, dispersed costs" phenomenon. It describes the fact that members of Congress, as political entrepreneurs, concentrate their benefits on special interests, which as a class represent a comparatively small group. But the costs of such benefits are dispersed throughout the whole taxpaying population. The behavioral effect is that those who benefit do so greatly and are, therefore, inclined to reward their representatives substantially. Conversely, the citizens who bear the costs of such favors are affected insignificantly and are not, therefore, inclined to protest.

This fiscal/behavioral phenomenon is not new. In fact, Pareto, the Italian political economist, described it in 1896.[3] Pareto asked his readers to imagine a country of 30 million inhabitants in which it was proposed, under some pretext, to get each citizen to pay out one franc a year and to distribute the total amount among 30 persons, giving each a million francs annually. Pareto asked: How would the two groups differ in response to the situation? They would "differ very greatly," he predicted. The potential gainers of the 1 million a year would "know no rest by day or night." They would "win newspapers to their cause," discreetly "warm the palms of needy legislators," having their agents "descend in swarms on the electorate, urging the voters that sound and enlightened patriotism calls for the success of their modest proposal," and "lay out cash to get the necessary votes for returning candidates in their interest."

But how about the individual who is "despoiled" of one franc a year, as Pareto put it? He "will not for so small a thing forego a picnic in the country, or fall out with useful or congenial friends, or get on the wrong side of the mayor or prefect. In these circumstances the outcome is not in doubt: The spoilators will win hands down."

More recently, Arthur Burns, former chairman of the Federal Reserve Board, expressed similar thoughts.

> The potential beneficiaries of a spending program are often a numerical minority, but they have a stronger incentive to keep informed, to organize, and to lobby for their favorite program than those who bear the cost have to oppose it. The rising cost of political campaigns and the concurrent proliferation of fund-raising committees put intense pressure on legislators to vote for spending programs favored by such groups. We may, in fact, be entering an era in which governmental processes are overwhelmed by the naked demands of increasingly well-organized and effective interest groups.[4]

The advantage that the Alphas and Betas have over the Significant Others, then, is due to several reasons. For citizens, it is simply not worth the time to fight back to save a few dollars. But for members of Congress and interest groups a lot is at stake. For the former reelection may ride in the balance, for the latter a good share of their income. Citizens are diffused, unorganized, and physically spread around the whole country. The Alphas and Betas, by contrast, are localized in Washington, concentrated, and highly driven. The costs to the Significant Others are not immediately known, but to the Alphas and Betas the political and economic benefits are immediate and real. It is only natural, then, that members of Congress respond to pressure groups whenever they come asking for money. And because unlimited deficit spending makes that possible, the electoral power of each is enhanced, and at the expense of the Significant Others.

THE DISADVANTAGED PAYERS

The focus in this section, as indicated previously, is on the role of fiscal illusions in reducing citizens to the position of Significant Others in electoral power, while at the same time making it easy for Congress and special interests to become the Alphas and Betas of it.

Fiscal Illusion Defined

The word "illusion" is used here in Webster's sense as "something that deceives or misleads intellectually." Fiscally speaking, then, we are talking about modes of financing that deceive or mislead intellectually.[5] Two situations illustrate the point. In the first, fiscal illusion is kept to a minimum; in the second, it dominates the exchange.

In no real-world setting where money is exchanged for goods and services is fiscal illusion totally absent, but a free marketplace comes as close as any. Most of the elements for dispelling fiscal illusions are there, allowing customers to make reasonably rational decisions about costs and benefits. Take a supermarket as an example. Prices are clearly marked for every product, which is absolutely essential for comparing costs and benefits. Product information is also present. Labels describe contents, give instructions regarding use, and carry warnings where appropriate. Comparison shopping is possible, either with products on the same shelf or with those in another supermarket. At the checkout counter there is a direct exchange of money for merchandise. Further, there is a record of the sale, usually in the form of a tape, should any question arise later. Finally, there is usually an understanding that should a product be defective, the store will make good.

Here then is a setting where fiscal glasnost prevails, narrowing considerably the opportunity for fiscal illusion.

Compare this store, now, with the congressional "store" where government goods and services are "sold." Instead of dispelling fiscal illusions, it creates them, leaving the customer-taxpayer with little or no basis for making rational judgments about costs and benefits. For example, there are no marked prices, and there is little product information. Comparison shopping is impossible, since the congressional store is a monopoly. The method of payment, a tax, is ambiguous; it bears no relationship to the products or services provided. There is no record of "sales" tying the cost to the product. There is no recourse should the product prove defective; Congress is not known for making good on its failed programs and services.

Consider, now, the illusions that this fiscal order creates. Hidden prices encourage the illusion that cost is unimportant; only benefits matter. A method of payment unrelated to the goods and services provided encourages the illusion that somebody else must be paying. Since the congressional store does not allow competition, the illusion is encouraged that the goods and services offered are the best available and for the least money. The overall effect is to "deceive or mislead intellectually."

PUVIANI ON FISCAL ILLUSION

Let us now enlarge the concept of fiscal illusion with some historical perspective. Like Pareto's notion of concentrated benefits and dispersed costs, the concept of fiscal illusion is not new. Indeed, one of the early proponents of the idea was an Italian contemporary of Pareto, Amlicare Puviani. Written down near the turn of the century, Puviani's ideas were at first largely ignored. Later, however, he was "rediscovered" and his works gained deserved recognition. Political economist James M. Buchanan introduced Puviani's work to English readers in several of his writings.[6] I am indebted to these for the following observations about Puviani's conception of fiscal illusion.

Like many of those historical figures whose voices were recalled in essay two, Puviani was a political realist. Important political choices, he believed, were made by the ruling classes of his time, leaving little genuine participation for the people. The idea that governments serve the general interests he found unconvincing. Puviani did not believe, however, that their antidemocratic actions were deliberately designed to serve their own self-interests. They were taken, instead, for pragmatic reasons, to keep social friction at a minimum.

It was out of this realism that Puviani constructed his hypothesis about fiscal illusion. All fiscal acts of government, he postulated, should be seen as intended to do two things: hide their true costs from taxpayers and magnify their benefits. Again, however, Puviani was careful to state that these acts were not deliberate. But — and here is Puviani's main point — when governments succeed in these attempts to hide individual costs and magnify benefits it is because fiscal illusion helped them to do so. They create the impression that costs are less than they really are and that benefits are greater than, in fact, they are.

Having stated his hypothesis, Puviani went on to explain how governments created fiscal illusions in the imposition of taxes. He mentioned five such ways. First, governments that have large incomes from the public domain — for example, socialist states, which own the means of production — use those revenues to defray the costs of government. The illusion left with the people is that those costs are much less than they really are. Excise taxes, which are buried in the price of products, are the second way in which governments create illusions about costs. In purchasing such products individuals are unaware that they are also paying for government or by how much. Public debt, Puviani said, was the third way that governments create fiscal illusion about their actual costs. Because the costs are pushed forward in time, most citizens are unaware that there will be a day of reckoning. For that reason public debt makes government goods and services seem almost free.

Of all the fiscal illusions, inflation, Puviani asserted, is the most illusionary. The reason? Most citizens are unaware that in cheapening the currency and raising prices the government at once collects more money in taxes and effectively reduces the amount of its loans. "Here," interjected Buchanan in his account of Puviani, "the public is clearly hoodwinked, and it has been through the ages."[7]

The final way that governments generate fiscal illusion is by making false promises. Spending programs, for example, may be promoted as being small, temporary, and inexpensive, but they end up being large, permanent, and very expensive. A new tax may be described as "temporary"; inevitably it becomes permanent. The result is that the taxpayer is subjected to ever increasing costs in perpetuity.

FISCAL ILLUSIONS IN MODERN DEMOCRACY

Puviani's Italy at the turn of the century was governed by an elite ruling class that no one would describe as democratic, and it was their revenue system he wrote about. Does the concept apply equally to a democracy, where people, in some ultimate sense, rule?

The answer depends upon one's view of what it was, exactly, Puviani was describing. Was he speaking of behavior unique to a particular kind of government? Or was he describing human tendencies present in any kind of government? In other words, is it in the interest of all rulers, regardless of the type of government, to minimize costs and maximize benefits? The question may also be extended to the ruled. Will people be less susceptible to fiscal illusions under one type of government than another?

These questions cannot be answered with any precision, but if one thinks democrats are immune to fiscal illusion he or she might take another look at our own federal tax withholding system. Begun during World War II as a convenience to taxpayers, it is now an established institution that few would want to change. Were Puviani alive, however, he would likely regard it as a classic example of fiscal illusion in tax collection. By focusing the taxpayer's attention on what is left after taxes, it diverts attention away from what is paid in taxes. The result is an illusion about the individual's share of the cost of government. Evidence of that may be seen in the reactions of taxpayers themselves. For many, the really important question is not how much they paid, but how much they will get back. Paying for the costs of government has almost become a "cash back" deal, in which the real costs are downplayed almost into insignificance.

Suppose the impossible, however, that upon some pretext this mode of collecting federal taxes at the source were abolished and everyone had to go back to the old system of writing an annual check each spring for the whole amount. How would individual perceptions about the costs and benefits of government change? Would there be less illusion or more about the individual costs of government? Would citizens be less or more tolerant of proposals to raise taxes? Would they be less or more likely to communicate their feeling to Washington? In short, would they feel more or less empowered with respect to the revenue system? The human tendency seems clear. With fewer fiscal illusions they would likely feel a need to exert more direct control over it.

And how about the members of Congress? Would they be more sensitive or less to the cost/benefit ratios of government expenditures? Would they feel a greater or less need to prove the case for higher spending? Would they be more forthcoming or less regarding the real costs of government?

The point is simply this: Our fiscal order dictates far more than how money is collected and spent. It has a lot to say about who is Alpha, who is Beta, and who are the Significant Others. In the very way it favors tax spenders over taxpayers it opens the gate for money to overwhelm the electoral process in the way Congressman Vento described.

Table 3 is an attempt to summarize in graphic fashion the several strands of thought running through this discussion of fiscal illusion. It relates the three modes of financing the costs of government to three variables: the amount of illusion, citizen electoral power, and Congress/ interest group electoral power.

TABLE 3
Mode of Finance, Fiscal Illusion, and Electoral Power

Mode of Finance	Relative Amounts of Fiscal Illusion	Relative Amounts of Electoral Power	
		Citizens	Congress and Special Interests
Direct Taxation:	Least Illusion	Most Power	Least Power
Debt:	More Illusion	Less Power	More Power
Money-created Inflation:	Most Illusion	Least Power	Most Power

Direct taxation, it will be noted, evokes the least fiscal illusion of the three modes of financing the costs of government. For that reason citizens are in a position to exert the most democratic control over it. At the same time, Congress and special interests derive the least electoral power from it.

Debt financing has more illusion, because citizens do not receive a tax bill for current costs. Their electoral power is, therefore, decreased. But for Congress and special interests it is increased.

Finally, since money-created inflation evokes the greatest fiscal illusion, it gives Congress and special interests the most electoral power and citizens the least.

To summarize: Our fiscal order is better designed to undermine the people's electoral power than nourish it. In concentrating benefits on the few and distributing the costs among the many the people's voice is effectively stilled. In avoiding taxation, which evokes the least fiscal illusion, and instead embracing debt financing and money-created inflation, which evoke the most, the fiscal order ensures that electoral power will increasingly flow from the "hands of the people" to the "pocketbooks of the few" and "megabuck" campaigns. I repeat: Modes of government finance are far more than ways to pay for the costs of government. They determine who are the Alphas and Betas of electoral power and who are only Significant Others.

Woodrow Wilson once remarked that "money being spent without taxation and appropriation without accompanying taxation is as bad as tax-ation without representation."[8] Today we have precisely the condition that the former president warned against. We have representation without taxation, and that is as bad for the democratic order as the other away around.

9 The Budget Process: A Design for Debt

> As long as any legislative body . . . can give different interest groups who ask for money what they want, write checks in red ink, and avoid responsibility — human nature being what it is, the legislative body will yield to that temptation.
> — Senator David L. Boren

Senator Boren's observation about the connection between human nature and red ink in legislative bodies[1] evokes a number of interesting questions, all worth exploring. In the first part of this essay, I shall focus on one: How does the congressional budget process make it easier to yield to the fiscal temptation the senator from Oklahoma describes? How does it facilitate giving interest groups the money they want, writing checks in red ink, and avoiding responsibility?

The viewpoint presented here begins in an assumption about the relationship between human beings and the rules they create for the institutions they inhibit, whether those are families, businesses, or government. That assumption is this: They fashion institutional rules to fit their collective private desires. To know the rules, then, is to learn something more about the people in those institutions. Conversely, to know the people is to understand better the rules they insist upon.

That assumption finds affirmation in the budget-making process of Congress, and in two ways. First, when examined for its underlying fiscal intent, the process reveals itself as much more than an administrative tool for producing annual budgets: It is an elegant instrument of deficit spending, making possible exactly the kind of fiscal behavior Senator Boren describes. In other words, it fits the members perfectly, and the members fit it in the same way. Second, the members have scuttled every proposed reform that would have made it more difficult to "give different interest groups who ask for money what they want" by writing checks in red ink. Were this prerogative not important to them they would not have consistently violated their own voted efforts at reform. I shall, therefore, discuss both the spending biases built into the budget process and the failed efforts to reform it.

The second part of this essay extends the previous essay's concern for the way debt has an impact on representative government. The question focused on there is this: How does the members' ability to "give different interest groups who ask for money what they want, write checks in red ink, and avoid responsibility" affect the way they govern? I find that it distorts democratic practice, and in six critical ways.

RED INK MADE EASY

Consider now some of the unstated ways in which the budget process makes it easy to yield to the fiscal temptation the senator points out. The cumulative effect of these, it can be seen, makes annual deficits a near certainty.

Expenditures and Revenues Are Treated as Separate and Unrelated Matters

In most private households, spending proposals and income must be considered together. "Can we afford it?" states the organic link between the two. In the budget process of Congress, however, they are practically alien considerations. And as if to make sure that they stay that way, they are handled by separate committees, each jealous of its own prerogatives and turf. The family that assigns certain of its members to spend money and others to make it, with instructions not to let one influence the other, would be acting in a manner consistent with the way Congress makes its budget.

Revenues, It Is Assumed, Expand to Meet Expenditures

This is an assumption private householders wish they could make but cannot without courting financial trouble. With Aristotle, they know there is a "boundary fixed"; it is exceeded at one's own risk. Congress, however, acknowledges no boundary fixed. It need not, for increased expenditures can always be covered by further borrowing.

No Running Totals of Proposed Expenditures Are Kept

A family that refuses to look at the current balance in their checkbook before making further purchases would feel quite comfortable with this feature of the budget process. Only after each legislative committee has developed its "want list" is the question of how to pay for all of them raised. And, of course, that is the responsibility of yet other committees.

Spending Priorities Are Irrelevant

The appropriations committees act on each legislative committee request without regard to their relative merits. A family usually has to ask priority-type questions like: "Will it be a new car this year or a new roof?" But in Congress questions of comparative need seldomly get considered seriously. All requests are assumed to have equal merit.

All Requests Are Considered Worthy of Being Funded

The money committees of Congress — Ways and Means in the House and Finance in the Senate — are, as a matter of course, expected to find the money, one way or another. The annual deficit, then, automatically becomes the difference between tax revenues and the sum of all requests. Family members who routinely expect their every demand for money to be met, somehow, are acting in the spirit of the budget process.

Requests That Cannot Be Covered In-Budget Are Funded "Off-Budget"

If the money committees fail to fund spending proposals, frustrated members take the "off-budget" route. The fiscally frustrated family member who breaks the budget with a credit card spree would be responding in a similar fashion.

During these years of tight budgets, off-budget spending has increased dramatically, and not only because it is another way to get the money: It has certain positive advantages. Here are three of them. Off-budget expenditures receive little or no scrutiny before being approved. They are usually authorized without a dollar, or time, limit. And annual funding is usually automatic.

A prime example of off-budget spending is "tax expenditures," so called because, being in the nature of deductions, deferments, and exemptions, they "spend" tax money before it ever gets into the national treasury. The growth of tax expenditures has been phenomenal, nearly twice the rate of federal spending. For taxpayers not so favored, of course, there is a big catch. They must pay more taxes so that those with tax expenditures can pay less.

To repeat, these fiscal biases suggest that the budget process is far more than a set of procedures: It is a facilitator of political desire and a guarantor of federal debt. By assuming that revenues automatically rise to cover increasing expenditures the process makes borrowing a certainty. By considering expenditures separately from revenues it makes for the same result. By not keeping running totals it almost assures unbalanced budgets. Without priorities, it forecasts excessive spending. In expecting the money committees to fund every request, it denies them their traditional watchdog functions. And in allowing huge off-budget expenditures, the budget process itself becomes a fiscal charade.

And how does the budget process allow the members to "avoid responsibility" for writing checks in red ink? The answer is found in the process's complexity and convoluted procedures. They provide perfect cover for the members. No ordinary citizen, even if given the time and money required, could possibly untangle the lines of personal responsibility for the debt among the more than 160 committees and 535 members. The responsibility for deficit spending is not only spread around; it is buried in anonymity.

Consider next Congress's longtime resistance to attempts to reform the budget process.

Reforms Rebuffed

Over the years, groups in Congress have attempted to reform the budget process. In their repeated failures we see revealed the depth of the majority's addiction to the type of fiscal behavior described by Senator Boren.

A bit of history lends perspective to these efforts. Until early in this century, Congress prepared its own budgets, debated and passed them, and then sent them on to the president, who would either veto or sign. In 1921, however, Congress decided that the executive should prepare the budget and send it to Capitol Hill for action. That has been the procedure ever since. At the beginning of each new term the budget is prepared by the executive branch and transmitted to Congress for its disposition.

In 1946, Congress decided to take a more active hand in the budget process. The Legislative Reorganization Act of that year called for a legislative budget in addition to the one prepared by the president. The purpose, Congress said, was to better reflect its own economic priorities. One of the key provisions of the 1946 act was a requirement that Congress put a ceiling on expenditures. Though the act passed by a substantial margin, it was that limitation that doomed it to failure. In the clutch, Congress refused to set a limit on its spending before it had considered its members' pleas for money. A foe of the measure, Congressman Clarence Cannon, chairman of the House Appropriations Committee, declared, "We can no more expect success with this well meant but hopeless proposal than we can report a verdict from the jury before it has heard the evidence." This first serious attempt to bring expenditures in line with revenues died aborning.

In 1949 Congress made another effort at capping expenditures. In the Omnibus Appropriations Bill all the money requests were brought together into a general spending bill. For the first time the members could consider all requests together. The bill also placed statutory limitations on spending, keeping them in line with revenues. Like the 1946 attempt, this reform also failed.

The Budget Control Act of 1974 constituted a more impressive effort. It provided Congress the opportunity to set spending ceilings and related spending to income and both to the total financial need of the federal government. Strictly a process act, it was revenue-neutral, neither encouraging nor discouraging spending. Its only intent was to give Congress a more informed basis for making budget decisions. It passed with resounding support, 401 to 6 in the House and 76 to 0 in the Senate.

This act established new players in the budget game. It created new budget committees in each house and charged them with guarding the public purse. They were to monitor both revenue and spending legislation, keep running totals on spending, and conduct "early warning" sessions in which revenue and appropriations bills would be reviewed for their impact on the budget. With respect to setting spending ceilings, the budget committees were directed to produce two budget resolutions each year, one scheduled for adoption before spending and revenue legislation was considered and the other shortly before the start of the fiscal year. The first resolution set tentative targets for both spending and revenues. After Congress approved the second resolution it was not supposed to violate its self-imposed budget restraints.

But, again, it did. As in the past, the sticking point was Congress's inability to set limits on spending and stay within them. At first, however, it appeared that it might. For several years after 1974 the first nonbinding budget resolutions were passed, so also the second, binding, ones. Then cracks began to appear in the solid consensus that had voted the measure into being. The binding resolutions were violated; even the nonbinding first resolutions became a point of bitter contention. Finally, in 1985, Senator Kennedy pronounced the act's obituary. Said he: "The budget process is in a shambles, the deficit is out of control, and Congress is part of the problem."

The historical record seems to justify this conclusion: These efforts at reform failed not because they were unneeded, but because they were unwanted. They would have made it more difficult for the members to have the excess funds required to "give different interest groups who ask for money what they want, write checks in red ink, and avoid responsibility."

And that reality brings us to this question: How does Congress's insistence upon this practice distort representative government?

DISTORTIONS IN REPRESENTATIVE GOVERNMENT

In a perceptive essay titled "Whither Democracy?" F. A. Hayek contrasted two types of legislatures.[2] The differences between them, he believed, hinged on these two matters: how they use their power and where they get their support. The first type uses its power to intervene in people's lives by conferring special benefits on some groups and imposing special burdens on others. Its commitment is to favorites. The second type, on the other hand, is more interested in fairness than favorites. It limits its lawmaking to what Hayek called "universal rules of just conduct." It uses its power to regulate competing interests, mediate among them, work out compromises, and shape agreements that may not please all the combatants but reckon well with the rights of everybody.

As to where they get their support, Hayek argued that legislatures that limit their authority to providing equal treatment find broad support in public opinion, because citizens recognize that the rules apply equally to all. Such legislatures can be trusted. On the other hand, those that regard their power to intervene as unlimited purchase support by granting special favors to special interest groups. They cannot be trusted.

This practice of officials in all-powerful organizations selling favors is not, of course, new. Indeed, it is very old. Recall, for example, those corrupt priests of the medieval Christian church. Their favors were called indulgences, and they sold them as pardons for sin. These opportunistic divines, having arrogated to themselves power over men's souls, began to think that they could reward with paradise or punish with purgatory. Salvation no longer depended upon universal rules of just conduct; it could be purchased for a price. Financial clout, not merit, became the test for determining who would be admitted through the pearly gates or cast into the murky depths of hell.

And what happened to the moral authority of the church during this tragic period? It became seriously eroded. Unlimited power, unchecked by principles of universal just conduct, became predictably oppressive, reactionary, and corrupt.

The current distrust of Congress does not arise in trivialities, as one might conclude from some cartoon caricatures. It goes far beyond the comic. Borrowed money in hand, Congress stands astride the gates of opportunity, dividing the winners from the losers on the basis of who can deliver the most campaign money and votes.

Consider, then, six ways in which the sale of congressional indulgences distorts representative government.

First, it distorts the very reason for governing, which becomes not to govern well, but to govern for political profit. The commitment of the corrupt priests of the church was not to nurture a sacred trust, but to exploit it. The church had become for them a means, not a valued end in itself. One strongly suspects that government may have become that for some members of Congress. Its value is not in its inherent worth, but in its personal utility.

Second, when the reason for governing is political gain, it follows that government itself becomes one huge indulgence to be sold to the best advantage. As an indulgence, government has myriads of attractive forms, like cash subsidies, tax expenditures, loans, grants-in-aid, and numerous entitlements. Taken together, these indulgences constitute a very substantial part of government, all of it available for sale in exchange for support. And, of course, at somebody else's expense.

The third distortion is that the majorities required to pass laws become mere fabrications of special interests. Majorities in a democracy ought to represent a genuine consensus. And they do, when their purpose is to enforce universal rules of just conduct, rather than to reward special interests. But when indulgences pass for laws, the nature of the majorities supporting them alters radically. They become merely the means by which separate groups of interests buy support from one another at the expense of unwitting others. Such majorities have no more in common

than a pledge to vote for someone else's pet project in exchange for votes
for one's own. Members may not even know what is in a bill; they only
know that if they do not vote for it, their own indulgences will be
threatened or denied. In truth, majorities fashioned in this manner are
more like institutionalized blackmail. They are a corruption of the true
meaning of majorities as valid expressions of public opinion.

Long ago Socrates refused to dignify the actions of such majorities
with the name of "law." He called them "decrees" instead. Legislation
that did not apply equally to all, that favored some groups at the expense
of others, was of men, he said. He did not want to live under that kind of
government.

The fourth distortion presents a paradox. It is that all-powerful
legislatures that refuse to limit their authority to universal rules are in fact
weak. And the reason is that they are wholly dependent for support on
splinter groups that are held together only by the favors congressmen
command. Congress needs them, for they create the market for
indulgences. Without these splinter groups, there would be no one to sell
favors to.

Common Cause likes to describe ours as a "Special Interest State,"
which indeed it has become. But the way it all began is frequently
overlooked. It started not in public demand, but in congressmen's need to
sell indulgences. That came first; they created the market for the special
interests. Publicly, congressmen may malign and curse special interests,
but government by indulgences would collapse without them. Once that
reality is fully grasped, the origins of the "Special Interest State" become
clear. It was conceived in Congress, and it will be sustained by Congress
so long as it has indulgences to sell.

The Special Interest State also has a darker side: coercion. Since
indulgences favor certain groups at the expense of others, one would not
expect those penalized to pay voluntarily. They must be compelled to,
through coercive taxation. Without this coercion, then, the system of
indulgences would collapse. So, when Congress sells indulgences to
special interest groups it also sells them the right to coerce other citizens
to pay for their benefits. Coercion is part of the deal.

Fifth, the sale of indulgences encourages government waste and
inefficiency. Former senator Proxmire's "Golden Fleece" award became
the symbol of senseless waste in government. But his graphic and well-
documented indictments did not explain why Congress has this
compulsion to waste. The implication was that the cause was only bad
management or careless trusteeship. It likely is neither. Waste is a
requirement of those who regard government as one big indulgence to be

bartered away for votes. The rewards are not in being efficient, but in being profligate.

I come, now, to what to me is the gravest distortion of all: social justice. There is a great irony here, for indulgences are commonly given in the name of social justice. In truth, most go to the middle and upper classes, rather than the poor.

How has social justice come to this perversion? No one, I believe, has analyzed it any better than Bertrand de Jouvenel, the French political philosopher. Invited by Cambridge University to give its esteemed Boutwood lecture, de Jouvenel chose as his subject the ethics of redistribution.[3] Tracing the history of who is helped, and who is hurt, by such politically inspired programs, de Jouvenel concluded: "The more one considers the matter, the clearer it becomes that redistribution is in effect far less a redistribution of free income from the richer to the poorer, as we imagine, than a redistribution of power from the individual to the state . . . the greater gainer from which is not the lower income class as against the higher, but the state against the citizens."[4]

Everything considered, it would appear that Hayek was right. A democratically elected assembly that uses its unlimited power to "confer special benefits and impose special burdens on particular groups" must buy its support from numerous special interests. And that price for most citizens is dear.

SUMMARY

Social institutions, psychologically speaking, are the projections of the private needs and wants of the members who inhabit them. To know the rules, then, is to know more about their members. Similarly, to know members is to understand better the rules by which they are governed.

In this essay I have attempted to view the fiscal desires of the members of Congress through their budget process and the implications of that for the way we are governed. The view confirms that there is a strong symbiosis between the fiscal implications underlying the budget process and the political desires of the members who created it. They have fashioned a process that makes it easy for them to indulge different interest groups, give them the "money . . . they want, write checks in red ink, and avoid responsibility." And an examination of the failed attempts to reform the process reveals the depth of the members' commitment to keep it that way, even at the expense of the way we are governed.

10 Voices from Within: Congress on the Debt

> In candor, I must . . . say to my colleagues that Congress itself seems to lack any will or strategy to limit and then eliminate the deficit under present procedures.
>
> — Senator Edward Kennedy

When the long history of the debt is written, a few brief weeks in the fall of 1985 may stand out as the most revealing and prescient. That was when Congress, quite unexpectedly, debated the Balanced Budget and Emergency Deficit Control Act, or Gramm-Rudman. Never before had there been a debate on the debt quite like it. It was far more than an argument over a measure to balance the budget: It cast serious doubts on Congress's intentions to do it, ever. It was in this skeptical atmosphere that Senator Kennedy spoke his doubts in the quotation above.[1]

Looking back on it now, that debate takes on new significance. It forecast the fate of Gramm-Rudman. It reaffirmed the central role of Congress in the problem. And, perhaps most important of all, it brought into sharp relief two very different models of government, federal and state. That contrast came about in this way. A number of the participants had been, before going to Congress, elected officials in states where balanced budgets are mandated by either statute or constitution. Their arguments are of a unique character, standing out from all the rest. Not only did they understand firsthand that balanced budgets work; they were very clear about which type of budget produces the better form of government. They confirmed again that the core issue of the debt is not money; it is the way we are governed.

The model of congressional government that emerges from the debate is that of a national legislature habituated to debt, unable to break the habit, incapable of making tough choices, dependent on special interests, and increasingly removed from rank-and-file citizens. In contrast, the model that emerges from state government is that which we associate with a vigorous and vital democracy. Priorities are set, hard choices made, and budget promises lived up to. One suspects that the difference between the two is accountability. Balanced budgets require elected officials to be accountable. Unbalanced budgets do not.

The plan for this essay is as follows: In the first part the warning signals from the Gramm-Rudman debate are recalled in the words of those who spoke them, and with a minimum of comment from me. In the second part, former state officials speak their minds on both the feasibility and the influence of mandated balanced budgets. The essay closes with a brief summary analysis of what has gone before.

CIRCUMSTANCES PRECIPITATING GRAMM-RUDMAN

A good place to begin the discussion is with the circumstances that precipitated the Gramm-Rudman debate in the first place. Throughout the seventies and especially in the first half of the eighties, the debt had annually escalated to new highs. Escalating, too, was public alarm over it. Congress, it was becoming clear, had to do "something." But it was an immediate circumstance that put the fat in the fiscal fire. The Treasury was running out of money, and it was urgent that Congress raise the debt ceiling to an unprecedented $2 trillion to enable the government to borrow more money to pay its bills. Historically, raising the debt ceiling had become a routine affair, almost ritual, except for those members who used the occasion to protest mightily for the sake of the voters back home. But the outcome was never in doubt. The measure would pass, money would come flowing into the Treasury again, and spending would go on as usual.

Not this time. The supporters of debt reduction balked. They would not vote to raise the debt ceiling to that astronomical figure, they gave their colleagues notice, unless Congress at the same time passed a debt reduction bill, and one with "real teeth" in it. That proviso was important, for on numerous previous occasions Congress had airily passed such measures and then just as breezily forgotten them. Gramm-Rudman, however, would not be that easy. First, it called for a target date for eliminating the deficit: 1991. Second, five annual installment payments were required. And third, there were real penalties for not meeting those payments. Should Congress default, automatic, indiscriminate, and

across-the-board cuts would be triggered by the president —
sequestering, it was called. Fiscal decisions would thus be taken out of
the hands of Congress. That was the real sticking point. For the first time
in history Congress would be required to either balance the budget on its
own or have a sequester do it.

What happened, of course, is history. Congress passed the act with
broad bipartisan support — it was the politic thing to do — but failed to
live up to its intent. In order to avoid sequesters the books were annually
juggled to make it appear that installment payments had been met when,
in fact, they had not. And, as of this writing, Congress keeps pushing the
1991 target out into some indefinite point in future time. The ultimate fate
of Gramm-Rudman thus still hangs in the balance.

FIVE THEMES OF WARNING

When one sits down with the *Congressional Record* covering late
September and early October 1985 and pores over the pages of the
Gramm-Rudman debate, five warning themes appear and reappear. They
are:

Congress's uncontrollable urge to borrow and spend,
Congress's use of deficit spending for political advantage,
Congress's lack of will to reduce or eliminate the debt (Senator
    Kennedy's theme),
Congress's violation of its own statutes for balancing the budget, and
Congress's inability to be fiscally responsible unless forced.

In focusing on these particular themes from the several weeks of
argument I do not wish to imply that they either dominated the debate or
represented majority opinion. But they were far more than "asides," too;
they were persistent and determining undercurrents of thought. Nor do I
suggest that they were entirely free of political posturing, for many
members have mastered the art of campaigning against Congress in order
to stay there. Still, one finds in these arguments reasoned judgments
entirely consistent with those of outside observations. They deserve
thoughtful consideration.

Turn, then, to the first of the five themes and how it was voiced.

The Uncontrollable Urge to Borrow and Spend

For most private citizens borrowing is a periodic affair, usually
for "big ticket" items that eventually get paid off. Constant, repeated

borrowing to cover regular household expenses is reasonably rare. In the excerpts that follow members indicate that for Congress such borrowing is not the exception, it is the rule.

In the first excerpt, Senator Packwood of Oregon used an analogy to illustrate that point and its consequences.

Mr. President, we are on the debt ceiling bill, and just so that we might simply lay out what the debt ceiling bill is and why we are here to raise it, let me put it in illustrative and rather simple terms.

Assume that you have a country that has 12 people in it, and the Government promises to each of those 12 people that it will give them $100 a year — $1,200. We are going to pay that out of the coffers of the Government. We raise taxes enough only to produce $1,000. So we have promised to pay $1,200, we have collected only enough to bring in $1,000, and if we are going to bring in the $1,200, we have to get the $200 someplace.

What we have been doing is borrowing it. The Government can only borrow money with the authorization of Congress. So the President comes to Congress and he says, "Ladies and gentlemen of the Congress, please pass authority for the Government to borrow $200 so that we can have $1000 of taxes and $200 of borrowed money to pay each of our citizens $100 a year." We approve it. The year goes by. We pay each of the citizens their $100. The year is gone.

Now we are into the next year. We still have 12 citizens. We are still promising to pay them $100 a year. We are still only collecting $1,000 total. So next year we are going to pay out $1,200 and have only $1,000 coming in. Again we are $200 short. Only now we have already borrowed $200 last year and all we are paying is the interest on it. We are not paying back any of the principal.

So when we get to this year the President says again to Congress, "Ladies and gentlemen of the Congress, last year you authorized me to borrow $200 to pay for the difference between what we are paying out and what we are collecting in taxes."

We are borrowing that and we are borrowing it all the time because we are not paying anything on the principal. Now by the laws that you passed we are going to continue this process of paying out $1,200 and taxing $1,000. So now we need to borrow another $200 on top of the $200 last year. And if we cannot borrow it because we are not going to tax it and we are not going to cut the spending or have not, then we cannot meet our obligations. So he asks us to increase the debt ceiling from $200 which was the ceiling last year to $400, again because we are paying nothing on the principal. So we pass a law that says the President can borrow $400.

And that is what we have been doing year after year after year, and now we are at a situation where we have borrowed up to the limit that the law allows, somewhat in excess of $1.8 trillion. And as we are going to have a deficit in the magnitude of $170 billion to $200 billion the President has come to us and said, "Ladies and gentlemen of the Congress, will you please raise the debt ceiling the slightest," in excess of $2 trillion so that we can borrow the money to pay the obligations that we said we are going to undertake?

And Congress really has no choice and Congress is as much at fault in this as is the President, because we have passed the laws authorizing the spending. We have even appropriated the money for the spending and now we either have to tax it, borrow it, or renege on the promises that we made about this spending.

So we are here today on the debate on the debt ceiling. On occasion I am amused by some of my colleagues who will vote for most of the expenditures month in, month out, month in, month out, and vote against any taxes or enough taxes to pay for it, and when it comes time to vote for the debt ceiling to borrow the money make their one vote of the year in defense of fiscal conservatism by voting against the debt ceiling, having voted to spend all the money.

The time to stop spending is not when you have already promised to spend it all and appropriate it all and at the end of it go out to borrow it. The time to stop the spending is before you make the promise to spend it.[2]

Representative Koble of Arizona asked: "When are we going to face up to the tough choices that we have to make about spending?"

The problem is that Congress cannot control its own appetite for spending, and yes, we could grow out of this deficit if we would just restrain ourselves on the spending side; it would be possible not overnight, not in 1 year, but it would be possible for us to get ourselves out of this box if we could really control our spending appetite.

It seems to me that is exactly what Gramm/Rudman is all about. I have listened for the last several days to the national media, and read discussions in the newspapers and heard discussions on the floor of this body about all of the technical things wrong with Gramm-Rudman, and we need to look at those and make sure it is in the best possible condition that it can be. But the real issue that is involved, it seems to me, in the Gramm-Rudman amendment is a fundamental question: When is this body going to establish priorities in spending? When are we going to face up to the tough choices that we have to make about spending? When are we going to stop borrowing from our children and our grandchildren? When are we going to stop spending their inheritance in this country?[3]

Representative Walker of Pennsylvania focused on how Congress's uncontrollable urge to borrow and spend has an impact on the budget:

The problem that we hear so often defined on the House floor that is brought up with regard to the Gramm-Rudman proposal is the fact that somehow we are going to get away from what is Congress's responsibility to do budgeting.

Congress has had the responsibility under the Budget Act here since 1974. The fact is the budget process has failed miserably. It is coming apart at the seams; we have consistently, over the last several weeks, had rules out on this floor that were aimed not at enhancing the budget process but destroying the budget process.

Every bill that comes to the floor under a rule recently, it seems, has a waiver on it of the Budget Act. Simply throwing the Budget Act [out] and saying that we do not need that Budget Act any longer.

The reconciliation bill that we brought to the floor today is going to be voted on tomorrow, came out under a rule that waived the Budget Act. It seems to me that it is awfully strange to have a bill that is supposedly enforcing the Budget Act that has to come out here with a Budget Act waiver in it; there is something awfully strange happening in this House — and we all know what it is; it is a strange system of spending, spending, spending.[4]

Representative Craig of Idaho explained Congress's urge to borrow and spend in terms of the ease with which the costs can be passed to others "down the road."

The tough choices are hard to make most anytime . . . and the reason it is very easy to avoid them [is] because we can always go out and borrow the money, as we have historically done, especially in the last 20 years in growing dollar amounts on an annual basis, saying, "Well, somewhere down the road somebody else is going to have to pay for it."[5]

Representative Barton of Texas concurred with Mr. Walker.

The truth of the matter is that the budget means nothing. It is simply some procedure that we go through each year so that we can tell the public that we have met our responsibility of saying what we are going to spend money on and how much, and they believe us year after year, but they do not watch, because we hid it with those various supplementals that keep throwing the budget out of kilter.[6]

Deficit Spending for Political Advantage

The debate over Gramm-Rudman left little doubt about the political origins of the debt. If it were not an attractive tool for winning votes it likely would not exist. The three members whose comments follow make that abundantly clear.

Senator Gramm of Texas explained the politics of the debt in terms of a cycle that begins in spending other people's money and ends in requiring them to "pull the wagon."

What a wonderful world it would be if we could spend money and never have the bill come due. Wouldn't it be wonderful to have a magic credit card that would allow you to go out and charge, but nobody sends you the bill? We almost have it in Congress. We spend the money; we create constituencies; they vote for us; and then send the bill to the people pulling the wagon, while we load up the wagon.[7]

Senator Proxmire of Wisconsin traced the origins of the debt to a simple, straightforward fact: Deficit spending is "so much easier politically."

We should decide priorities. We should advance programs that have the highest priorities. We should cut programs that have lower priorities. We should aim for overall spending and deficit reduction. If we fail in making the cut big enough we should increase taxes to make up the difference. That is what we should do. But oh it is so much easier politically to vote for every spending program, showing each and every interest group, and our public constituency, that we agree with their specific spending priorities.[8]

Senator Thurmond of South Carolina explained the politics of debt in much the same way as Senator Proxmire. The members can reap the "political benefits of . . . spending . . ." he said, "without having to place themselves on record for higher taxes to pay for such spending":

This spending bias arises from the fact that Members of Congress are free to vote for new spending initiatives without, at the same time, having to vote for new tax initiatives. In other words, Members of Congress can vote to support the programs of the spending interests, and reap the political benefits of such spending — in the form of electoral support, for example — without having to place themselves on record for higher taxes to pay for such spending. There are no countervailing political disadvantages in the form of tax votes that would overcome the political advantages stemming from the pro-spending votes. . . .

Because of the unlimited availability of deficit spending, Members of Congress are free to respond favorably to the spending groups without having to vote for the necessary new taxes to pay for their new programs. Rather, Congress can merely indulge in new deficit spending. The consequences of such deficits come only in future years — in such forms as inflation and interest rates — and are rarely attributed to the Members who voted for the earlier deficits. In other words, Members reap the benefits of the prospending vote and avoid totally the need for the protaxing vote. It is a case of Members eating their cake, and having it as well.[9]

Lack of Will

The most pervasive single theme running through the Gramm-Rudman debate on the debt was Congress's lack of "will" to do anything about the problem. Spoken sometimes in sadness, it was, nevertheless, a reality widely acknowledged, and by veteran members on both sides of the political aisle.

Many, like Senator Kennedy of Massachusetts, would have preferred other ways to reduce the debt, but supported Gramm-Rudman, since Congress showed no will to address the problem on its own.

> Mr. President, I prefer the Democratic leadership alternative and I have voted for it. But with its defeat it is also clear to me that we could argue endlessly about how and when we will balance the budget without making any real progress.
>
> The Gramm-Rudman approach has its problems and I hope and expect the House of Representatives will amend it to begin the process of deficit reduction now and to finish it earlier. But we can hardly say that we oppose balancing the budget later because we cannot pass a bill to balance the budget sooner. In candor, I must also say to my colleagues that Congress itself seems to lack any will or strategy to limit and then eliminate the deficit under present procedures.
>
> In August the Senate voted for a budget that promised a deficit of $172 billion. It was a fraud then and there were those who said it was. Now the deficit has risen about $20 billion in just 2 months.
>
> The only thing in recent years equal to the record Federal deficits is the fervent rhetoric heard in this Chamber about the urgency of a balanced budget. I would reach the goal faster and in a different way, but I believe we must reach it.
>
> I would rather restrain spending by picking the weakest or most wasteful programs not by across-the-board cuts. But I also believe we must have cuts. . . .[10]

Senator Hatfield of Oregon opposed Gramm-Rudman for the same reason that Senator Kennedy favored it. He saw no point in passing a new measure to pay off the debt, "no matter how cleverly contrived . . . unless we summon the will and courage to make it work. I do not yet discern that change of will":

> Mr. President, I oppose this proposal. No matter how we dress it up with modifications and fine tunings to meet the specific objections or interests of one Member or another, it remains a fundamental unsound proposal that again represents a congressional abdication of its fiscal responsibilities. . . .
>
> Mr. President, it is not easy to defend the status quo. There is not much worth defending. But I am convinced that our current predicament lies not so much with the present congressional budget process as with our will to make it work, and no new system, no matter how cleverly contrived, will work unless we summon the will and courage to make it work. I do not yet discern that change of will. We are only fooling ourselves, and worse, fooling the people, if we believe this proposal will bring order out of chaos and put us on a sure path to deficit reduction.[11]

Senator Heinz of Pennsylvania found Congress's lack of "political will" to act on the debt a matter of "profound concern."

> It should be a matter of profound concern to all of us that a failure of political will has brought us to the point where we must reform the budget process in order to force ourselves to act. It is like the killer saying, "Stop me before I kill again." Although this is not the preferred method of legislating, the fact is that we have run out of options.[12]

Senator Weicker of Connecticut was sure that Congress had all the power it needed now to cut the debt. What it lacked was the "guts" to do it.

> The question has to be asked, do we have the power right now to reduce the deficit? Could we raise taxes? You bet your life that we are able to do that. We did that the last several years while all of this was going on. We can do it but do not do it. We could cut defense spending. We do not do it. Or we could reform the entitlements. We do not do it.
> All the power is here right now to do what needs to be done.
> But I will tell you any other piece of legislation that comes down the pike, whether it is this or a balanced budget amendment or line item veto, it's a legislative substitute for the guts which we do not have to do what needs to be done. It is as simple as that.[13]

The bluntness of Senator Weicker was more than matched by Representative Smith of New Hampshire.

> The truth of the matter is that we, collectively, we, this congress, does not want to balance the budget, has not wanted to balance the budget, and probably will not balance the budget without something like the Gramm-Rudman, which gives us, as has been said, earlier, the discipline and the will to do it. . . . I think the American people ought to take a good look collectively at all of us and individually at all of us and say, "Let's call a spade a spade, and let's lay it on the line, folks. You don't want a balanced budget, you want deficits, you want debt, because that is what you are voting for."[14]

Violation of Own Statutes

While Gramm-Rudman was a major attempt to balance the budget, it was by no means Congress's first such attempt. A number of members, remembering past failures, were skeptical about Gramm-Rudman. Would it be just another instance of Congress's failure to live up to its own promises?

Representative Craig of Idaho voiced his skepticism in this way:

It was this fear and this concern and a lack of willingness to make hard, tough fiscal decisions that brought me to the conclusion some time ago that it would not be a law inside this body; that it would not be a Federal statute that would and could control the spending of our country. . . .

My argument and the argument of a good many others who support Gramm-Rudman is that it will not solve the problem. It is telling the American people by law, by legislative action that here is a process, here is a 6-year process that the American public can watch and that will govern this body and the other moving toward a balanced budget by 1991.

Remember, it is important to recognize that it is a law; it is not a constitutional amendment, it is a Federal statute if it becomes law.

It was in 1978 and 1979 that this body and the other body in their wisdom passed similar laws that said, by a given date — and that date was 1981 — that we would have a balanced budget; that we would require of our Government to have a balanced budget; in essence, we would require of ourselves a balanced budget.

What happened? Why do we not have a balanced budget today if it is in fact law upon the books of this country that we were to have one by 1981?

Sadly enough, there lies the problem. What laws this body passes are laws that it can change; and it decided, as it found that it was very difficult to cut spending, very difficult to bring budgets in balance, that it would simply violate the law by ignoring the law with another law; and of course in the Budget Act and in the rules of the House, that became an easy kind of thing to do.[15]

Senator Grassley of Iowa, in view of these failed legislative attempts to balance the budget, regarded himself as "once bit, twice skeptical."

Mr. President, I support the stated purpose of the amendment — offered by Senators Gramm and Rudman: That future spending must be reined in, and that the Federal budget must be balanced in the foreseeable future.

However, Mr. President, I have reservations about this legislation, not only in terms of its ability to balance the budget, but also in the way it has evolved over the last 2 weeks.

First, in terms of its effectiveness: The changes outlined in this amendment are not ineffective in and of themselves. For me, it is a case of being "once bit, twice skeptical." In 1978, Congress passed a law known as the Byrd-Grassley law which mandated that no deficit spending could occur beginning in fiscal year 1981. That is now a public law.

Well, obviously, we have not only deficit spent every year thereafter, but since 1981, we merely doubled the trillion dollar debt.

Mr. President, for the past 5 years, Congress has willfully ignored a statute mandating a balanced budget. What makes us think Congress will balance its budget as a result of this amendment? Or any other bill? The problem doesn't require new legislation because the law is not the problem.

We do not need legislation with teeth in it. Congress would still do what it wills, with or without teeth. The problem is the will. It's the unwillingness of Congress to commit to self-discipline.

There are two activities involved in self-discipline. The first involves realism, which requires us to recognize how bad the current crisis is. The second involves hard decisions to limit spending. If we do not first recognize the size of the problem, the decisions for cutting spending will be inadequate.

Congress chooses optimism over reality precisely so that our decisions will be less disciplined. This has been the pathology of our failure to control deficits.

If there is one truism that supersedes all others where the Federal budget is concerned, it is this: The results of our decisions never match up with what we planned. It is this fundamental precept which compels us to view this amendment with a strong dose of realism.[16]

Inability to Be Fiscally Responsible Unless Forced

The need to force Congress to act responsibly was a continuing theme throughout the debate. And many members thought it would take something stronger than the Gramm-Rudman, for example, a constitutional amendment or presidential line-item veto. Senator Hefflin of Alabama was convinced that only a constitutional amendment would provide Congress with the "willpower to cut Government spending and balance the Federal budget":

Mr. President, the first bill I introduced as a Senator in 1979 proposed a constitutional amendment to balance the Federal budget. Since that time, I and many of my colleagues have worked to formulate a consensus approach to curb Federal spending. In the 97th Congress, the Senate did pass a constitutional amendment to balance the Federal budget, but Congress as an entire body has yet to enact this vital legislation. Unfortunately, the Houses' failure to pass this amendment has only allowed the Federal deficit more time to increase at an alarming rate.

It is with a sense of frustration and urgency that I rise today to introduce Senate Joint Resolution 7, a Senate joint resolution once again proposing a constitutional amendment to require the Federal Government to achieve and maintain a balanced budget.

I am convinced that Congress and the administration do not have the willpower to cut Government spending and balance the Federal budget without a constitutional amendment providing the discipline to do so. Maybe, as some argue, there is no need for a constitutional amendment, but the helter-skelter fiscal irresponsibility demonstrated within the past 25 years indicates otherwise.

For much of the history of this great Nation, a balanced Federal budget was part of our "unwritten constitution." In the first 100 years of this Republic, a balanced or surplus budget was the norm. There have been periods in our history when the exigencies of war or recession have necessitated operating the budget with a deficit — but initially there were always attempts to balance the lean years with the more prosperous ones. In the past two decades, however, Americans have seen higher and higher levels of deficits, taxes, and spending. Legislators tend to look at each program separately, not realizing that every dollar appropriated becomes part of a larger debt, a debt that is threatening the economic stability of our Nation.

In 1789, when the Constitution was adopted, Thomas Jefferson warned, "The public debt is the greatest of dangers to be feared by a republican government." Somewhere we lost sight of our forefathers' admonitions.

In 1963, 174 years after the adoption of our Constitution, the national debt was $300 billion. Today, as we begin the new year, 1985, the total Federal debt is $1,622,966,000,000. It has taken less than 25 years to more than triple our national debt. Currently, on an annual basis, we are operating at a deficit of approximately $200 billion. If we continue our current course, it will take less than 5 years to double the existing debt. . . .

I am convinced that we can no longer use the simple rhetoric that we, as elected officials, will do our best to control Federal spending. Our best is not good enough. Elected officials are constantly bombarded with requests from different organized lobbyist groups to help one program or another. Well, it is time we listened to a larger lobbying group — a group that while not as well organized is just as powerful and just as worthy of our attention as any other lobbying group — the American taxpayer.[17]

Senator Danforth of Missouri argued that such proposals as a constitutional amendment would not be "my first choice for reducing the deficit. My first choice would be responsible congressional action. But Congress has not shown itself to be willing . . . to take such action."

Mr. President, the Gramm-Rudman amendment is long and complex, but the question before us is very simple: Are we going to take decisive action to eliminate the enormous Federal deficits that threaten the strength and stability of the nation's economy?

At the beginning of this year we all agreed that the times could not be more propitious for a major reduction in the Federal deficit. The American people had just reelected — by a landslide — a President identified with spending cuts. The economy, while not robust, was strong enough to make reductions in Government spending possible. The effect of the deficit on interest rates and on the value of the dollar was creating serious difficulties for American agriculture and other sectors of the economy that are sensitive to international trade. Congress could consider the budget free from election-year politics. The Republicans in the Senate committed themselves to setting the budget on a course toward balance in 1990.

And yet, with the confluence of all of these favorable factors, we labored mightily and brought forth a mouse. We made some progress against the deficit, but we fell far short of the targets we set for ourselves. The truth is that we let the country down.

I am a cosponsor of the proposed constitutional amendment to require a balanced Federal budget. I am a cosponsor of legislation to provide the President with temporary line-item veto authority. And I am a cosponsor of the Gramm-Rudman amendment before us today.

I cannot say that any of these proposals represents my first choice for reducing the deficit. My first choice would be responsible congressional action. But Congress has not shown itself to be willng and able to take such action, and it is for that reason that I support the institutional constraints that have been proposed.[18]

Finally, Senator Proxmire defended his support of Gramm-Rudman in terms of the force it would apply to Congress to balance the budget, though he did not align himself with either a balanced budget amendment or a presidential line-item veto.

Mr. President, there is overwhelming criticism by newspaper editorial writers, by columnists, and by the country's outstanding economists of the effort the Congress is making to provide some kind of mandatory framework that will force the Federal Government to bring our budget under control. The criticism is wise and thoughtful. It is also dead wrong. What both the House and Senate are doing in mandating spending reductions seems harsh, arbitrary, and unfair. Why? Because it is harsh, arbitrary, and unfair. It is also necessary.

Mr. President, you have to serve in this body for several years to understand that, because we have to go back to our constituents to be reelected, we will not cut excessive spending of popular programs, unless we have to do so. We will not raise taxes, unless we are forced to do it. Those of us who serve here have learned that. That is exactly why the U.S. Senate, by an overwhelming 3-to-1 vote, decided against the advice of the country's most thoughtful observers to put these severe restraints into effect.[19]

What significance shall we attach to these skeptical voices from within Congress? It would probably be easy both to over- and under-estimate their importance. Or to write them off as political posturing, since the possibility exists that the skeptics themselves are part of the problem, talking prudence but practicing profligacy. Even if that were so, the real significance, I believe, lies elsewhere.

What we observe here is the culture of federal debt and the extent to which it has insinuated itself throughout the institution of Congress. As Senator Gramm said, "We spend the money; we create constituencies; they vote for us; and then send the bill to the people pulling the wagon." The debt, then, is not a reasoned thing. One listens in vain for a single voice in rational defense of it. All one hears is defense of expenditures that create it.

FISCAL BEHAVIOR AND BALANCED BUDGETS IN THE STATES

What stands out in references to state budgeting is the different sort of fiscal behavior that balanced budgets require. It stands in sharp contrast to that in Congress, where no limits on spending are imposed. One can only conclude that balanced budgets encourage fiscal responsibility, while unbalanced budgets breed fiscal irresponsibility.

The following dialogue between Representatives Barton and DeLay, both of Texas, illustrates the point. The need for a balanced budget encourages Texas state legislators to set priorities, make tough decisions, and practice effective oversight on expenditures.

> *Mr. Barton*: "The question I would like to ask the gentleman from Texas is, since he did serve in the Texas legislature and the Texas legislature does have a balanced budget requirement, was there ever a year that people requested less money than there was available to spend?"
>
> *Mr. DeLay*: "Absolutely not. Members would come with their own little special interests and they would ask for more money. But the body as a whole had to sit down and prioritize based upon how much money they had in Texas that next year or that next biennium, and they would have to prioritize these programs and turn down some good programs, turn down some increases, and yet move the money around so that we only spend as much money as we take in."
>
> *Mr. Barton*: "Were those decisions and those choices easy to make?"
>
> *Mr. DeLay*: "Never are they easy to make. I think that is much to the credit of the legislators that serve in the Texas legislature. They constantly are showing the courage to stand up and make the right decisions."
>
> *Mr. Barton*: "Was the gentleman from Texas ever totally satisfied about the choices that were made on how to spend the money that was available?"
>
> *Mr. DeLay*: "Absolutely not, never satisfied, because I never got what I wanted and many other members never got what they wanted. But I think the people of Texas got what they wanted."
>
> *Mr. Barton*: "That is my point exactly. If the Congress of the United States, like the Legislature of the State of Texas, is forced to make choices, the people will get what they want because there will be a tremendous give and take and priority decisions will be made and, in the absolute, the available funds will be spent in the most effective fashion and on those uses that the majority of the people support."
>
> *Mr. DeLay*: "I might say, if I can, another great outcome of this in the State of Texas is that members watch how the money is spent, with a lot more favor, because they want to make sure that the money they did get is spent to its ultimate efficiency. So they spend a lot more time watching how the agencies spend that money. So that is another little extra that you get out of living under a balanced budget."[20]

Senator Hollings, former governor of North Carolina, pointed out that Gramm-Rudman was "not a wild, untried scheme. . . . When I was Governor of my State, it worked well then, and while it could be in some Member's mind a little cumbersome, the cumbersome nature is not such a burden as the burden of the $2 trillion debt itself."

Mr. President, in the early days of the budget process, I would have liked to present my own version of a balanced budget along with Senator Muskie — because we as former Governors, in creating the budget process — thought we ought to have some teeth in it. As Governors we had developed a balanced budget approach before and it is a working thing that can be done. There is no use to look at the Federal Government and say it is an impossibility. If there is an impossibility part of the Government, it is the Congress; it is that the Congress does not want to do it.

So we want to entice and encourage and persuade as best we can all of our colleagues on both sides of the aisle — as I say, do it or work it out — and make sure that there is a mechanism instituted to balance the budget that we can live with.

Mr. President, the plan we offer today might be better entitled the "Truth-in-Budgeting Act." It will once and for all remove the politics and the finger pointing from the Federal deficit. It will enable us to cut away the rhetoric and get to the task at hand by providing us with the discipline that we are so sorely lacking to make the budget process work.

We have tried several ways to win the discipline of both Houses, of both parties, at both ends of Pennsylvania Avenue, and the fact is that with all this so-called great leadership and wonderful Congress and wonderful executive branch and everything else, the national debt is about to exceed the numbing figure of $2 trillion. That, to me, is the most convincing argument that the discipline needed to make the budget process work is simply not there.

It is time to let realism take over. It is time to let the truth take over. And it is time that the measure we offer today is put into effect so that we can bring about exactly that, truth in budgeting.

It is not a wild, untried scheme. It is one that the overwhelming majority of the States — 43 to be exact — have in effect right now. Some have it in their law, some have it in their constitution, some have varied ways to approach it. But, in essence, this is something that members of the legislature in both parties in all sections of the country experience each year.

We experienced it earlier this year in my State of South Carolina. Our distinguished Governor, acting under the State's Budget Act, had to make a percentage cut across the board because we are suffering from high unemployment and the exodus of our industry overseas.

When I was Governor of my State, it worked well then, and while it could be in some Member's mind a little cumbersome, the cumbersome nature is not such a burden as the burden of the $2 trillion debt itself. So now is the time for us to go to work and bring some kind of realism.

Let us bring into the Nation's Capital what is practiced around the nation, and expose the budget to the budget process so that we can get the job done, enable the Federal Government to live within its means, and then solve all of these related problems — namely, the trade deficit problem, the industry productivity problems. It is an outright disgrace when we politicians travel the country and belabor industry — that American industry should compete, should become productive — that we in Congress by our assorted politics, and failure to have truth in budgeting, actually exact anywhere between the 30- and 40-percent burden or tax on that productivity in the industry itself. No matter how productive they become we are going to make absolutely certain by these high deficits and the overvalued dollar that would be the result — that they will be burdened with 30 to 40 percent.

Failure to do this will only shift more and more debt to the generations ahead of us, and undermine the economic strength of the Nation.

Mr. President, what we in reality are doing is pulling in the credit cards with this particular amendment to the debt limit. I urge my colleagues to join me in sponsoring the measure.[21]

Senator Boren, former governor of Oklahoma, described in some detail the fiscal behavior that the balanced budget requirement called for in his state.

Mr. Boren: "When I was Governor of Oklahoma, Mr. President, I operated under a system that was similar to Gramm-Rudman. There was a State board of equalization which was made up of State officials, including the budget director and the Governor, which prepared estimates of the anticipated revenues, estimates of the costs of programs that we had enacted, then they followed and tracked all the figures as they came in. If our estimates were over our projections, if they were too rosy, if the money we had expected did not come in or our expenditures went out too quickly, we had no choice; in our case we had to balance the budget.

Just as under this proposal, we had to meet the budget deficit targets that are set out in this particular piece of legislation.

What happened was that if we failed to meet our targets, by automatic operation of the law, there was an across-the-board cut in everything. That meant in my operation of the Governor's office, if I were operating that office with a budget of, say, $1 million and I had to experience a $50,000 cut as a part of an across-the-board-in-all-functions-of-government cut; I had to sit down and figure out how I was going to operate the office with $50,000 less.

I can tell my colleagues this system works. It works. We faced the situation in my State just a few months ago. As all of us know and my colleagues have heard me talk about the agricultural economy and the oil price impact on the energy sector, we had a very difficult time in my State. We had a shortfall of revenues and could not continue our programs at the usual level. What we did is, we had to make some across-the-board cuts.

The raises which policemen and teachers and others were looking for were not going to be able to take place. We had to take immediate action rather than hoping for a more productive economy.

What did we have to do? The Governor had to call the legislature back in session. They had to decide: Do we want these automatic cuts to go across? Did they want teachers not to get any raise? Did they want the road program cut, the corrections program cut, other education programs cut? They had to decide.

In the case of our State legislature and the Governor, they decided, yes, they would live with some of the cuts. In other cases, they decided that some of those programs were so vital that they would raise the revenue necessary for those programs and keep them in operation. In other words, they had the opportunity to meet their responsibilities.

I heard somebody the other day talking about this proposal. He said,

> This proposal is terrible. It puts us in a box. Do you realize that if we do not meet our budget deficit reduction targets, we will face the terrible choice of either having to cut programs or raise taxes to pay for them? We might either have to cut defense or raise the money to pay for the defense programs we think are important to the country. We might even have to cut some of the COLA's [cost of living allowances] or raise the money to pay for some of the COLA's.

Mr. President, that is just the box that the American people and the taxpayers have been hoping and praying to put this Congress and this administration in for many, many years. And it is time we got put in that box, for heaven's sake.

Mr. Hollings: "Amen."

Mr. Boren: "It is time we were put there. It is time we had to face up to our responsibilities. How in the world do you think we can balance a budget? There is only one way to balance a budget when you are spending more than you take in: You either have to cut back on what you are spending or increase your income.

I realize that is a radical statement here, in Washington, DC, because for some years, we have been balancing the budget with mirrors. We have canceled expenditures we have not even made yet. We have changed our estimates of economic growth.

It has been so long since people here realized how you really balance the budget, that you cannot do it with smoke and mirrors and resolutions about waste, that they have forgotten you either have to raise your income or cut your spending.

Well, put us in that box. Throw us in that brier patch. It is time we got in there and dealt with the real problems that are facing this country. That is exactly what this proposal does. That is why so many people want to squirm and squeeze and wriggle and find a way out of it. We are finally going to have to ask the American people — it is not only the Congress and the President that need to be put in this box. Truthfully, it is the American people as well. It is our fellow citizens. So when they come in and ask us for a program — maybe it is worthwhile — we can turn around to them and be honest enough to say, "We don't have any money to pay for it. Now do you want this program, American citizens, do you want it badly enough to pay for it or not? If you want it badly enough to pay for it, then that is the only way we can get it because we don't have the money."[22]

SUMMARY ANALYSIS

The implications that flow from the Gramm-Rudman debate are far-reaching and not a little disturbing. The supporters of the measure hinged their hopes on its enforcing mechanism. It would require the Congress to be fiscally responsible. If the members would not reduce the deficit on their own, a sequester imposed by the president would. That threat was to provide the "backbone" to make the "tough decisions"; it would overcome the "lack of will."

It did not. The debt continues to escalate. Promises continue to be made. The target date continues to be set back. The most skeptical of the 1985 skeptics in Congress turned out to be right. Had Congress really wanted to reduce, then eliminate, the deficit, it could have done so long ago, and without Gramm-Rudman. It patently does not want to.

What, then, should we do? Two things, I believe. We should first of all face up to reality and acknowledge that the chances of Congress ever voluntarily cutting the debt are bleak. Both historical and psychological evidence support that conclusion. We may wish it otherwise, but barring some unforeseen change in Congress, an honest assessment counsels healthy skepticism.

Second, we can let that reality generate within us as citizens a constructive, rather than cynical, response. This is no time to exit the political process; that only makes matters worse. The impasse over the debt can be a time of democratic renewal and emancipation, if citizens see it as an opportunity to create a new fiscal order in keeping with our open political order. The fiscal order suffers not from too much democracy, but from too little. If the Gramm-Rudman debate makes one thing clear, it is this: The nation's fiscal affairs are far too important to be left exclusively in the hands of professional politicians who think only of the next election. Their repeated failures have amply demonstrated that. Not only do we get bad fiscal policy; worse, we get bad government. The time is at hand, I believe, to democratize the fiscal process as we have the political process. If the debt problem can cause us to rethink both citizens' rights and responsibilities in respect to paying the costs of government it may turn out to have been a blessing in disguise. Some thoughts on how to use the debt to advance fiscal democracy in keeping with political democracy are presented in the final essay of this series. The political psychology of the debt can be altered, I suggest, if ways can be found for the people's voice to be effectively heard.

11 A New (Fiscal) Imperialism?

> The feudal landlords and their kind who came to rule over India had a landlord's view of the world.
> — Nehru

Few men in history were in a better position to describe imperialism than Jawaharlal Nehru, the first prime minister of independent India. Not only did he spend much of his life struggling against imperialism; he was jailed for considerable periods of time because of it. While in prison, he used his reflective mind to explore the character of imperialism and especially its human dimensions. Fortunately for us, he committed some of his thoughts to paper.[1] What draws the contemporary reader to Nehru over a half-century later is only in part his eyewitness perspective on imperial India; it is, rather, the timelessness of his concept of imperialism. He saw it as much more than one country's despoilation of another; that was but a consequence of something much deeper and more profound. Imperialism, Nehru believed, is a state of mind — "a landlord's view of the world," he called it. It exists whenever and wherever the existing order may be described as similar to that between landlord and tenant.

And it is this insight of Nehru's that slips the bonds of time and place. Imperialism is not only an age in history. It is also an attitude of mind, a bias capable of insinuating itself into the body politic at any time and place.

Congress's imposition of a huge and burdensome debt, and particularly without the expressed consent of the governed, qualifies, I believe, as a new form of imperialism, fiscal imperialism. The fact that the burden is imposed by elected representatives rather than old-time feudal-minded imperialists should not surprise. It only demonstrates the truth of Nehru's point.

WORRISOME PARALLELS

If evidence is wanted to support this conclusion, one need only point to the striking and worrisome parallels between our current regime of debt and that of the older imperialism. Manifestations of a landlord's view of the world are evident everywhere, just as they were during the age of imperialism among the great powers.

Consider first the nature of the arguments used to justify the debt. Any form of imperialism needs justification, for some liberty is lost, some means of livelihood denied, some restrictions imposed, some new burden mandated.

The colonial powers used two sets of justifications, one the acceptable, public one, the other the private, real one. Public justifications focused on opposites, the inherent deficiencies in the native populations and the natural superiority of the would-be masters, to correct those deficiencies. Endowed by sterling qualities and skills, the dominant powers were not only able, they were obligated to "protect" and "civilize" those not similarly endowed.

Privately, the old-style imperialism was motivated by self-interest. It was profitable, frequently fabulously so. Creating captive markets, it made trade monopolies easy. Competition was thus eliminated. Raw materials produced in the colonies at low prices flowed into the "mother" countries to be processed into finished goods and sold back at high prices. As a result, local manufacturing stagnated and withered away, thus making the colonies' presumed inferiority become self-fulfilling prophecy.

The old-style imperialism is mostly history now, but its lessons are instructive still. Its public justifications were false and its private ones self-serving. The deficiencies attributed to subjects were dehumanizing, its claim to superiority deceiving. Not only did it fail to correct the deficiencies; it helped create them. It was the cause, not the cure.

And what of Congress's justifications of debt? That too points to deficiencies in the economic and human condition. That too assumes the natural superiority of borrowed money to correct these deficiencies, a claim entirely lacking in evidence to support it. But evidence, or the lack of it, is not the real point. The central fact is that deficit financing is politically profitable. It creates loyal new constituencies, broadens the base of support, and eliminates competition. Each new claimed deficiency that comes along provides just one more opportunity to exact a political toll. Though the record is strewn with failed efforts, that is unimportant. Political gain is what counts.

Another theme that ran through the old-style imperialism also has its counterpart in our regime of debt. It has to do with holding onto power once it is attained. The device used by colonial powers was the creation of a permanent dependency within the colonies, an incapability for managing their own affairs. It had three faces: economic, political, and personal.

THE THREE FACES OF DEPENDENCY

Economic dependency was accomplished mostly by sucking away capital and economic surpluses from the colonies and channeling them into the mother country's economy. High taxes, price fixing, and trade monopolies made accumulation for growth impossible. Denied the capital to grow, the colonies became abjectly dependent on the economy of the imperial power.

In making the subjects dependent upon them, the great powers set loose a downward economic spiral from which many of the former colonies have not even yet fully recovered. The age of colonialism was not one of relieving the ills. It was, instead, one of arrested development leading to tragic economic consequences.

The awful famines of India were an example. They were created to no small degree by feudal-minded landlords who ravaged the land by stealing that which should have been returned to it in order to ensure future fertility. It was this deliberate policy of exploitation that kept India poor. In view of this stark experience, one must question the way the mounting debt drains resources away from badly needed programs for growth and development. Interest on the debt, debt-inspired inflation, and high interest rates all "steal" from the future, just as the feudal-minded landlords of imperial India did.

Another device to create economic dependency among the colonies also finds a parallel in Congress. The imperialist powers bought the loyalty of certain powerful special interest groups by granting favors not available to ordinary people. By sharing the spoils they bought control, and allegiance, of the elites and through them the masses. In India the favored ones were the great landed zamindars. Knighting them as rajahs and maharajahs, the British also gave them tax concessions, quite similar to what Congress euphemistically calls "tax expenditures." But by whatever name, the effect is the same. The favored groups pay less tax, the others more.

In sum, Congress, just like the old imperialists, creates economic dependency by shifting private capital, via deficit spending, to public ends for political purposes. Also like the imperialists, it buys, through a system of selective largess, loyalty to the regime of debt.

With respect to creating political dependency in India, the colonial bureaucracy was the main tool. Through complicated and obscure rules set in a foreign language, the bureaucracy controlled almost every aspect of Indian daily life. As subjects regularly queued up in long lines at colonial administrators' doors to state their grievances or seek preferment, they could not help but know who held the paramount power.

Ironically, the extensive employment of Indians also served to create political dependency. Though the positions available to Indians were low — mostly clerkships and menial jobs — the prestige of government service was high and the positions greatly sought after, because all other doors of opportunity had been slammed shut. Like the zamindars-turned-rajahs, these civil functionaries became good apologists for the imperialist system and soon took on the ideologies of the conquering power. They too began to see the same deficiencies in the masses as their masters did and began to claim superior qualities for themselves. In short, they also assumed a "landlord's view of the world." Alienated now from their own culture, they frequently developed an animus toward those ordinary mortals who had to pass in endless lines before them.

The vast bureaucracy created by Congress shows many of the same symptoms and performs many of the same functions as its colonial counterpart. Regulating many aspects of our daily lives, it constantly reminds us where the paramount power lies. Its employees, not unlike alienated Indians, became apologists for the system of debt.

Turn, finally, to personal dependency. In India it was created by denying individual freedom. Perhaps the most precious right taken away was the power of personal choice. Subjects were not free to aspire to be themselves or develop themselves, for survival itself depended upon assuming the biases of those in power. Thus while economic and political dependency exacted a high human toll, perhaps the highest toll was psychological, the demoralization that comes when one is denied control of his own destiny.

But in the long run the loss was not the Indians' alone. The colonial powers lost, too. In creating personal dependency among their subjects they denied themselves the creative human resources required to assure the future of almost every aspect of their colonial enterprise. In this they sealed their own fates by joining to economic and political stagnation human lethargy and ignorance.

A regime of debt also creates personal dependency. If one is the recipient of borrowed money he comes to depend upon it, even demand it. Addiction is not far away. But direct recipient or not, some control of one's future is lost, since public debt is in the end private debt, to be repaid in one way or another from future earnings. Ultimately it is the debt that, in effect, becomes the landlord and citizens, like tenants, must pay.

DEATH FROM WITHIN

What finally spelled doom for the old imperialists? Conventional wisdom points the finger at revolts and riots from within. But those only served to hasten the day. The rot had set in years before. It came in the destruction of productive capacity, in the denial of freedom to invest, to grow, to develop. Imperialism died within before it showed signs of demise from without. It finally collapsed in upon itself.

Imperialism's last years were both sad and instructive. Attacked from without, it had no power within to resist. All of its energies were absorbed in posturing and shoring up doomed defenses. As time went on, it became ever more punitive, rigid, and bureaucratic. Urges to change, to grapple with new reality, to look and plan ahead were lost in hectic and fruitless defensive maintenance. There was activity to be sure, but it was the frenzied kind, random, aimless, grasping. The great age of imperialism had come to an end in almost suicidal self-inflection. The revolters and rioters in the background only provided the discordant noises for the wake.

Are there warnings for Congress? I think so. Congress's constant obsession with borrowing practically precludes the development of vigorous and constructive programs of economic development. Its passion for immediate political gain wipes out any prospects for intelligent long-term planning. Its flight into debt only underscores its cowardice about going to the people to make the case for new taxes. The debt has thus become the new fiscal imperialism threatening the well-being of us all.

Will Congress change its fiscal behavior? And if so, how? These are the questions explored in Part IV.

IV WILL CONGRESS PAY OFF THE DEBT, AND IF SO, HOW?

12 The Political Psychology of Debt Retirement

> When national debts have been accumulated to a certain degree there is scarcely, I believe, a single instance of their having been fairly and completely paid.
>
> — Adam Smith

Will Congress prove Adam Smith right?[1] Or will it pay off the debt and prove him wrong? And if the latter, how? Those are the questions examined in this essay and the next. This one looks at the underlying political/psychological considerations. The next examines how these bear on four alternative scenarios for retiring the debt.

Is it possible, and solely on the basis of the political psychology involved, to predict what Congress will do? The assumption here is that it is not only possible, it is the only way to tell. Considerations like fiscal feasibility and economic desirability certainly give no clues. Had those motivated Congress the debt would likely have been retired long ago. Walter Lippmann's warning that "to talk politics without reference to human beings . . . is just the deepest error in our political thinking" applies equally to talk about debt retirement. To speak of it without reference to the human beings in Congress who must achieve it is part of the deepest error in our political thinking.

The reason for my confidence in this approach to debt retirement rests in those two powerful motivators of human behavior, pleasure and pain, about which Jeremy Bentham, the nineteenth-century British political philosopher, discoursed at such length. Political pleasure built the debt. Now we must test whether Congress is willing to bear the political pain of paying it off. The former was easy; the latter will be hard. And that may explain why Adam Smith, that astute observer of the fiscal affairs of nations, could scarcely recall "a single instance" when national debts, having "been accumulated to a certain degree," were "fairly and completely paid off."

PSYCHOLOGICAL KEY

The key to understanding the political psychology of debt retirement resides in the way pleasure and pain operate differently in public and private borrowing. They work to one effect in public debt and just the opposite in private debt. Once that reversal of incentives is understood, the psychology of the matter begins to reveal itself. To be specific: In private borrowing the pains involved work to constrain it and the pleasure comes when the loan is finally paid off. With members of Congress, however, just the opposite is true. The political pleasure comes in piling debt upon public debt and the pain in paying it off. In other words, the incentive system in private debt works to keep it in check, while in public debt it works to expand debt to excess.

Two implications arise immediately from this realization. The first is that much of the current criticism of Congress regarding the debt is, psychologically speaking, misguided. It mistakenly assumes that the members are, or should be, motivated by the incentive system of private debt and curses upon them if they are not. In reality, in piling one public debt upon another, the members are only doing "what comes naturally," and they apparently are not about to change.

The other implication speaks to proposals in Congress for retiring the debt. Any proposal that leaves intact the current incentive system will likely fail. Historically, they always have. To succeed, a proposal would have to realign the incentives more in keeping with those of private debt. Excessive borrowing would have to hurt politically, while paying off the debt would have to be pleasurable. Until that is done, nothing much about the debt will change, except perhaps its rhetoric.

Turn now to a more detailed look at how the incentive systems work in these two forms of debt.

PLEASURE AND PAIN IN PRIVATE DEBT

Anyone who has ever struggled to pay off a private loan knows both the pleasure and pain of it. My intent here is to go in search of the sources of these sentiments. Their origins, I believe, are to be found in certain hard and inescapable economic realities. For this reason I turn first to an examination of some of these realities. Here are five:

1. Private debt is an obligation to pay later for the use of money now; it is a claim against the borrower's current assets and future earnings.
2. Borrowed money used for ordinary household expenses — consumed, in other words — is borrowed money lost; it depletes the borrower's pre-loan net worth by the cost of the loan, and forever.
3. Borrowed money productively invested, however, maintains the borrower's pre-loan net worth, the exact extent depending upon the quality of the investment.
4. Borrowed money productively invested, and paid off from the borrower's current income, constitutes forced savings; it therefore increases the borrower's pre-loan net worth, and by the value of the investment.
5. Borrowed money paid off from additional loans, however, further depletes the borrower's pre-loan net worth, and by the cost of the new loans, plus interest compounded.

Two fictional middle-class families, whom I shall call Family A and Family B, will serve to illustrate these hard and inescapable economic realities of private debt. Similar in most respects, the two families were strikingly different in one: their behavior regarding these realities. And it is this singular difference that in the end made all the difference in their economic pleasures and pains.

Consider first their similarities. (I give these priority only to highlight the ultimate economic effect of their singular difference.) The two families consisted of the same number of adults and children roughly the same ages. They had the same number of income earners and about the same amount of disposable income. They spent most of what they earned, but each family was debt-free. Their homes were worth about the same, and their neighborhoods were of comparable socioeconomic status. They drove the same number of compact and mid-sized cars, also of comparable worth. In sum, the families were solvent, making it possible for each to provide their members with the basic necessities of life, plus modestly more.

Now, the difference. They both decided to borrow similar sums, but for quite different purposes. Family A placed a mortgage on their house in order to add a new bedroom, while Family B got a car loan to buy a new luxury sedan. (Their particular choices are irrelevant to the illustration except for what they represent in terms of the hard and inescapable economic realities of private debt.) In adding a new bedroom Family A made a productive investment whose value may fluctuate over time, but the chances are it will remain quite stable. By contrast, Family B put their borrowed money in a rapidly depreciating asset that, by the time the loan is paid off, will be worth only a fraction of what it was before. So, while Family A preserved their net worth through borrowing, Family B made themselves poorer, and forever, because they, in effect, consumed what they borrowed.

Another way to describe the two families' post-loan economic differences is in terms of single and double entry bookkeeping. Family A's condition may be properly represented by double entry accounting, Family B's by single. While Family A had to place the cost of the loan on the debit side of the ledger, they could offset that debit on the credit side with the value of the new bedroom. They balanced out. Family B, however, had only a rapidly decreasing asset to balance against the full cost of the loan. And in time that asset's worth would approach zero, a flat debit without a saving credit.

To this point, then, the behavior of the two families illustrates the first three hard economic realities of private debt. They both accepted the first reality, namely, that debt is an obligation to pay later for the use of money now. Beyond that, however, their behaviors diverged, and with predictable consequences. By consuming their borrowed money, Family B ultimately impoverished themselves by the amount of the loan, plus interest. But Family A, by investing productively, maintained their net worth, and possibly permanently.

After making their loans, the two families behaved differently in yet another regard. And that difference illustrates hard realities four and five. Family A made monthly payments from current income, in effect saved, by lowering their standard of living. Were they to follow that practice until the loan was paid off they would have increased their pre-loan net worth by the value of the new bedroom. Family B, however, chose another means of repayment. Opting not to lower their standard of living to make monthly car payments, they placed a mortgage on their house. As a result, their net worth became their pre-loan worth, minus the cost of the car loan, minus the cost of the mortgage, and minus the compounding cost of paying interest on interest. Further, Family B's economic condition can only worsen as the costs of debt service steadily mount. But even if their pre-loan assets were completely wiped out, the obligation would be unaffected; it would still be there to haunt them.

But the hardest reality for Family B may be yet to come: Their future options are now severely narrowed, or closed altogether — for example, a college education for the children. By shifting their debt burden forward in time, and thereby pre-committing even larger portions of their income to debt service, they drastically reduced their children's chances of getting a higher education. While Family A would likely not find it easy to send the children to college, they at least would have a realistic chance of doing so.

The Incentive System in Private Debt

Notice now how the incentive system works in private debt with respect to these hard and inescapable realities. It is almost as if there were within private debt a spontaneous psychological code that yields pleasure for those who manage it well and inflicts pain on those who do not. What, for Family B, began in a desire to improve their life-style could end up threatening their ability to provide the family members with even the basic necessities of life. Family A, however, followed a very different course. By lowering their standard of living to make monthly payments, by, in effect, putting these payments on a "pain"-as-you-go basis, they had something to celebrate in the end.

Now we must ask: What is the source of this spontaneous psychological code that yields pleasure for those who manage debt well and pain for those who do not? It is to be found, I believe, in the nature of the private debt obligation itself. That makes the difference; it accounts for why most private debts tend to get paid off. Consider, then, the nature of that obligation. First of all, it is serious. Spelled out in a written contract, the provisions are clear and the schedule of repayments definite. Second, the obligation is personal; it cannot be shifted to someone else. Third, the obligation requires repayment in a fixed period of time; it cannot be shifted forward without incurring more pain. Fourth, default is costly: Collateral would be lost, future credit jeopardized. Fifth, the obligation is permanent; even in default the pain of it lingers on. And, finally, getting rid of the obligation is pleasurable: What the borrowed money bought is owned free and clear, and the amount of the loan payments is freed up for other purposes.

It is the nature of the obligation, then, that gives meaning to the psychology of private debt retirement. It is not "good" in any abstract sense. The obligation is "good" because it counsels prudence in borrowing. It inflicts pain on the Family Bs of this world and reserves the pleasure for the Family As who manage debt well.

PLEASURE AND PAIN IN PUBLIC DEBT

When one compares the pains and pleasures of private debt with public debt, three things become apparent. Congress manages the public debt much in the same fashion as Family B did their private debt. The economic consequences are much the same, except for differences of scale. And, finally, in spite of these similarities, members of Congress suffer none of Family B's pains. Quite to the contrary: They even find political pleasure in them.

With respect to the management of its debt, Congress, like Family B, has used its borrowed money to up consumption. Instead of investing productively and repaying its loan from current tax revenues, it has depleted the nation's capital assets by the amount of the debt, now over $3 trillion and forever. Nobel Laureate in economics James Buchanan put the matter this way: "Not only has government failed to 'pay as it goes,' the government has failed to utilize productively the funds that they have borrowed. There has been no offsetting item of the asset side to match the increased net liability that the debt represents."

The economic consequences of this mismanagement now place Congress in the same precarious position as Family B. As the costs of debt service mount up, Congress finds it increasingly difficult to maintain even essential governmental services. And its future options are similarly narrowed or closed altogether. Resources to meet future needs may simply not be there. Future generations will have to fend for themselves, while still carrying the heavy burden of debt Congress has thrust upon them. Indeed, the current fiscal predicament in which Congress finds itself recalls to mind Aristotle's warning that only a solvent state can be a caring state. Might it be that Congress, years ago, when it borrowed its first dollar to increase public consumption, may have forecast the ultimate demise of its ability to provide for even the most basic of welfare needs? Current developments make that question more than academic.

Consider, finally, how, though the members of Congress manage their debt in the manner of Family B, and with the same dire economic consequences, they suffer none of Family B's pain. Indeed, they profit by it.

Why?

The answer will be found in the nature of the public debt obligation. That becomes apparent when it is compared with the private debt obligation. For members of Congress the public debt obligation is not at all serious in the sense that the private obligation is. It is not spelled out in a written contract, and there is no schedule for repayment. The obligation is not personal. The members are only agents, obligating us, not themselves, to repay the debt. And the obligation is not bound by time. It can, and is, shifted forward, endlessly and without penalty. Explicit default is not a threat; more borrowing, and taxing, will preclude that.

The obligation is in no way permanent; it is not even continuing, for other generations of congressmen, and constituents, are left to worry about it. And, finally, paying off the obligation is anything but pleasurable; it could cost members their seats in Congress.

In summary, I return to the question posed at the beginning of this essay. Will Congress prove Adam Smith right? Or will it pay off the debt and prove him wrong? The political psychology of the matter argues strongly for Smith. Of that there can be little doubt.

But let us suppose that Congress, because we are now in one of those "political breakpoints" in the ever escalating cycle of debt, feels the need to do something. What is it likely to do, given the incentive system described here? That question is examined in essay thirteen.

13 Four Scenarios

> Any decision to discharge or retire outstanding public debt must involve the imposition of sacrifice on current-period taxpayers and/or public service beneficiaries "in exchange" for promised benefits to be enjoyed by future taxpayers-beneficiaries.
>
> — James Buchanan

What future fiscal path will Congress likely follow with respect to debt retirement? Will it do nothing? Something? And if something, what?

In this essay I step back from Congress's almost daily protestations about the debt; I assume that they indicate little or nothing about what the members will, or will not, actually do. To understand that, I believe, one must first examine the psychological past and the human drives that brought us to where we are. Then one can ask: Has anything changed to foretell a different future?

Here I apply that question to four alternative scenarios for retiring the debt, examining each for the way in which it would satisfy, or deny, known and demonstrated political desires. On this basis I then suggest which of the four the members of Congress are most likely to follow. The prediction will not surprise: It is dour.

THE SCENARIOS

The following scenarios for paying off the debt are all plausible but only a couple possible and one, I believe, probable. They are:

Scenario One: Congress will pay off the debt, and in full.

Scenario Two: Congress will pay off the debt, but not "fairly and completely," to use Adam Smith's phrase; it will, in other words, default on some portion of it.

Scenario Three: Congress will not only default on some portion of the debt; it will simultaneously keep adding to it.

Scenario Four: Congress will cap the debt, in effect, "stop the fiscal bleeding."

The reader may wonder why I did not include explicit default among the scenarios, an outright repudiation of the debt. That indeed would be a bold stroke; overnight more than $3 trillion in debt would be wiped off the books.

Explicit default, however, is not a realistic option, either economically or politically. It would in an instant destroy the nation's credit, along with its credibility. Economically, it would be a devastating blow from which it would take the country years to recover, if indeed it ever would.

Politically, default is unthinkable, for it would place the whole burden for retiring the debt on a single influential group: the holders of the government's debt instruments. While many of these holders are foreign and cannot vote, most are U.S. citizens, who do vote. And many of these do more than vote; they also contribute heavily to political campaigns, both individually and through Political Action Committees. No incumbent member of Congress would dare incur their combined political wrath.

Further, there would be positive political advantages to spreading the costs of debt retirement across the entire population, whether those are in the form of increased taxes, higher inflation, or both. The costs per person would be dramatically less, they would be noticed less, and there would be less chance of political backlash. The increased taxes would be deducted at the source, and the increased cost of a loaf of bread would be blamed on the baker, not the local congressman or congresswoman. In sum, outright default will be avoided, somehow.

Two Assumptions

In these four scenarios I make two assumptions that should be noted here. I assume, first, that Congress will continue to have available to it the three historic means of all governments for retiring national debts. It can increase taxes, reduce expenditures, and/or print money and thus inflate the currency. Inflation amounts to implicit default, since holders of debt instruments are paid off with cheaper dollars than they originally

loaned the government. Implicit default is probably one of the means of
default Adam Smith had in mind when he spoke of national debts
scarcely ever being paid off "fairly and completely."

I also assume that the Federal Reserve Board, which regulates the
printing of money, though by statute independent of Congress, is not
entirely so. In the political crunch it feels the pressure "to go along."
Further, I assume that the "Fed's" ability to correct for the fiscal excesses
of Congress through regulating the money supply and interest rates is not
without limits. In the end, it is Congress that determines the level of fiscal
pollution in the economic air. The Federal Reserve acts only as the
protection agency with limited powers; it does what it can do to clean it
up. It does not control the polluters.

Scenarios Considered

In deciding which of the four scenarios Congress is likely to follow it
may be well to fix firmly in mind certain hard political realities about
public debt retirement. Then one can seek out that scenario that best
manages those realities and at least political cost. James Buchanan, in the
observation quoted at the beginning of this essay, points to two of the
most important of them. The first reality is the heavy sacrifice that is
imposed on "current-period taxpayers and/or public service beneficiaries."[1] Pleasure was the play in amassing the debt, but now it is time to
"pay the piper." There is no way out: If members of Congress are really
serious about paying off the debt, they must be prepared to impose
sacrifices on their constituents, either through higher taxes, reduced
government benefits, or both.

The second reality is that this onerous task must be done with the
weakest of motivational appeals: benefits for future constituents, not
the current ones required to make the sacrifice. In other words, the
members must ask present constituents, the ones upon whose votes they
depend to stay in office, to pay, as it were, for all the "sins of the fathers"
so that future generations may escape them. A tall order for politicians
who have built their careers by pushing current costs onto future
generations so that their current constituents would keep reelecting them.

What do these two realities suggest about the type of scenario the
members will likely choose? They will probably follow that course of
action that involves the least sacrifice and retains the most benefits
of deficit spending. In other words, the one that is closest to the status
quo.

Scenario One

In this scenario Congress would pay off the debt fully, and in real, not inflated, dollars. How politically like is such a scenario? Not very, and for one very good reason: The heavy sacrifice it would impose on "current-period taxpayers and/or public service beneficiaries," as Buchanan phrased it. With the debt now over $3 trillion, and rising, it represents a vast destruction of the nation's capital assets over a period of some 60 years. That $3 trillion can never be recovered, for it has already been consumed. But should Congress decide, as a minimum, to restore the balance in the nation's capital assets to what it was before borrowing began, it would have to extract that whole amount from current constituents. The resulting tax levies could only be described as confiscatory and the cuts in benefits as devastating. Politically, therefore, this scenario is about as unthinkable as outright default on the debt.

Recent efforts of Congress to retire the debt support this conclusion. Under Gramm-Rudman, for example, Congress was to reduce the deficit to zero through annual reductions between 1985 and 1991. It never made those reductions, except by doctoring the government's books to make it appear so. Gramm-Rudman sends a clear message that as yet seems not to be fully understood. The members of Congress are simply unwilling to suffer such large surges of political pain, and especially in relatively rapid succession. And the reason is because their constituents are unwilling to bear the economic pain that Gramm-Rudman would inflict.

I just suggested that the message of Gramm-Rudman is not fully understood. Permit me to elaborate, for the matter is of some importance. It speaks quite directly to public perceptions about the debt and its retirement. Put the matter this way: Suppose we knew an individual who vowed to pay off his debts. Suppose also that we knew that same person had a long record of not paying his debts. How would we judge that person's latest vow?

In assessing that vow we would likely look at it from various perspectives. Has he recently shown any genuine inclination to get out of debt? Has he really tried? How deeply has debt become an ingrained part of his nature? Are there signs of deep habituation? Does his life-style depend upon debt? And, most important of all, could he cope with withdrawal? Could he survive without debt?

Recall, now, that for six decades congressmen and congresswomen have symbolized that person. Yet we hardly ever raise those questions when they profess intentions to retire the debt. Instead, we quite blithely assume that when the members vow to pay off the debt they at least will try. What we tend to forget is that, as suggested in the previous essay, they operate on an opposite pleasure-pain code from private householders and nothing has occurred to change that. Until it does, not much about the debt will change.

The matter, I believe, comes down to this: In spite of Congress's 60 years of increasing addiction to debt, we still tend to think of a balanced budget as the norm and the debt still as a temporary aberration. What we have yet to appreciate is that in behavioral terms, balanced budgets are no longer Congress's norm at all. Unbalanced budgets are. Indeed, no living member of Congress knows what it is like to hang onto his or her seat under the political requirements of a balanced budget. Once we get that reality fixed in our heads, and firmly, we shall be better prepared to cope with the psychological barriers to debt retirement.

In expecting the current members to retire the debt, then, we are not asking them to return to a norm from which they temporarily strayed. We are asking them, instead, to break with a norm of which they have known no other. The request, in its behavioral effects, must be con-sidered no less than traumatic.

Scenario Two

Scenario Two would have Congress pay off the debt but, thanks to inflation, not "fairly and completely." This option has strong political appeal. Of all the ways to reduce the real dollar amount owed by government, inflation is the most politically inviting. It is quiet. It raises a minimum of political hackles. And the blame for inflation is deflected from Congress to the producers and marketers of consumer goods. Further, inflation, while it may devastate ordinary pocketbooks, fattens political ones in that there are more tax dollars to spend. And that means that constituents who are victimized by inflation can then be ensured against it by political appealing cost-of-living adjustments. Not to worry that this practice creates still more inflation: It creates more political supporters, too. Inflation as a political means is without equal.

But the other half of Scenario Two does have a catch. It still requires Congress to pay off the debt, albeit in nominal dollars. So, while the pain is reduced by inflation, it has by no means gone away.

How politically realistic is this scenario? Not very, if evidence from the decades of the sixties and seventies is any indicator. These were the years of double digit inflation, it will be recalled. As a result, the real dollar amount of the debt was slashed substantially, the reduction being borne by government bond holders who loaned real dollars but got back inflated ones. At the same time, of course, this inflation brought a flood of new tax dollars into the Treasury. So the question becomes: What did Congress do with all those new tax dollars? Did it use them to dampen down inflation by paying off the debt, as John Maynard Keynes might have recommended? The answer, of course, is on record. Congress followed its political desires instead. It spent the surplus on the "Great Society." The beat of the debt went right on.

In sum, Scenario Two, politically speaking, is bittersweet. While it allows Congress to default implicitly on the debt through inflation, a political plus, it still requires the members to pay it off, an action they steadfastly refused to take when given the chance.

Clearly, Congress wants it both ways. It wants a scenario that, on the one hand, reduces the real dollar obligations of government debt and, on the other, allows it the pleasures of deficit spending. And that is precisely what it gets in the next scenario.

Scenario Three

This is the scenario I believe Congress will most likely follow in the future, after we emerge from the "political breakpoint" we are currently in, perhaps around the turn of the century. Inflation is the magic key that makes this scenario probable. Through it the real dollar amount of the debt will be paid down, and yet it will allow Congress to maintain existing government benefits. And if inflation is high enough, Congress might even be able to lower taxes, too. A political grand slam. In short, all the sacrifice about which James Buchanan spoke is effectively avoided. And, of course, any real reduction in the debt. In real dollars, it will keep going up.

In retrospect, the sixties and seventies were a telling period in the study of the political psychology of debt retirement. They were, in a sense, a laboratory for viewing the operation of political desire when extra dollars become available. In those decades the political mood was expansive; there was no social problem money could not solve. It was also a golden age for enterprising politicians. Freed entirely of pre-depression balanced budget constraints, they could, as at no other time in fiscal history, follow their natural proclivities to spend. They might have used those inflated dollars to pay off the debt. But the siren song of political desire wooed them in quite the opposite direction: more spending, more debt, still more inflation.

My prediction is that Congress will, once the current pressures to retire the debt let up, return again to the fiscal practices of that period. The homing instinct will prove too strong to resist. They will go again in search of another political golden age, when the time in the political cycle is right.

Scenario Four

In this scenario, Congress would cap the debt at its current level, agree not to add to it, and carry the annual interest charges forward, like any other reoccurring expense of government. Politically, this scenario is possible but not probable, at least under the current expectations. In spite of the odds against retiring the debt, the public talk both in Congress and among citizens is of doing it. The debt is still something to be "paid off," testimony, no doubt, to the strength of the ethic of private debt in our society. Debt is simply not something that one walks away from. For this reason, Scenario Four has not found a supportive voice.

WHERE DO WE GO FROM HERE?

If these are Congress's options, and if my assessment of them seems reasonable, the chances of resolving the debt problem in our time seems bleak indeed. We would appear to be condemned to suffer ever-escalating levels of debt and all the personal and public pain that foretells. Can that pain be avoided? Can we, after 60 years of the debt habit, alter its fatally destructive course? In short, can we, at this late date, kick the habit?

We cannot, it seems clear, if we continue to try as we have in the past. The dreary, perennial escalating cycle must somehow be arrested and then reversed. To continue as we are is simply to assure disaster ahead.

From the opening essay I have tried to define the nature of the problem in a new way. I have suggested that the debt issue at its core is less about money than about how we are governed. Pay-as-you-go government, because it requires a new tax bill to be attached to each new spending proposal, is, by its very nature, more open, more democratic, and more honest than borrow-as-you-go government. In the latter, Congress secures its funding quietly, almost secretly, by simply voting to raise the debt ceiling. No political risks or hassles. No need to justify, explain, or defend with those who must ultimately pay. I have not argued that pay-as-you-go government would cost less than borrow-as-you-go government. Nor shall I, since the size of government is not the issue with which I am concerned. But the quality of government is. Borrowing releases in Congress forces of human nature that inevitably result in excessive debt. Worse, ordinary citizens who may see the federal debt as damaging to their own interests are practically helpless to do anything about it.

That reality takes us back to the necessity, not to keep on trying to find some superficial fiscal fix, but to realign fundamentally the relationship between the governors and the governed. My proposal, in short, is for a new fiscal democracy, one in which the people themselves have a more direct voice in how much is spent, what for, and how it is paid for.

We are living in an age of democratic revolutions. People everywhere are demanding a more direct voice in decisions that affect their vital interests. Yet, in the fiscal affairs of the world's oldest democracy that voice is effectively muted. The proposal presented in the next essay, the last, would increase the chances that most of those who ultimately must pay would be heard, and before, not after, the decision to spend is made.

V   A PROPOSAL
TO PONDER

14 Toward a New Fiscal Democracy

> No measure should be carried out unless it has the prior unanimous consent or at any rate overwhelming support of the people.
> — Knut Wicksell

As indicated in the preface, in writing these essays I thought of myself as taking an interested scholar's walk around the debt problem, sizing it up from various political/psychological points of view. Having now completed that self-assigned tour, I find one conclusion quite inescapable. It kept forcing itself upon me at every turn. That conclusion is this: Human nature, as it is currently allowed to operate unchecked in the fiscal affairs of Congress, not only encourages debt; it makes it almost inevitable. Worse, it makes getting rid of that debt almost, if not outright, impossible. Inescapable, too, is the implication that so long as that is the case, so long will the debt continue.

In this final essay, then, I take as my task this inquiry: Is it possible to change the way human nature currently works in the fiscal affairs of Congress? Can it be altered to give debt reduction a chance? A tall order, and perhaps impossible. But if we accept it as impossible we condemn ourselves to repeat the errors of the past. The times, instead, call for two qualities of mind that at first blush seem incompatible: a clear-eyed skepticism on the one hand and a determined optimism on the other. Such positive skepticism is the best antidote, I believe, for the political cynicism so prevalent today. The positive skeptic uses the way things are, as horrible as they may be, to see possibilities. The cynic pronounces a curse on "both your houses" and exits the scene. There is too much of that going on now. It is time, instead, to think creatively, plan wisely, and execute.

There is sound historical precedent for this kind of saving skepticism. From ancient times onward, political thought is marked by it. Aristotle, Adam Smith, and James Madison are examples. Each was a thorough-going skeptic about politics and human nature. But each made monumental contributions to thought about how to manage the problem. Aristotle began the tradition. "The avarice of mankind is insatiable," he said. "Men always want more and more without end. . . . It is in the nature of desire not to be satisfied and most men live only for the gratifications of it. . . . The greatest crimes are caused by excess and not necessity."

How would Aristotle check excesses in the state? Just as the well-ordered private household does, by recognizing the importance of living within "limits" and "scarcities." Only then could the state work for "the good condition of human beings." The answer lay not in accepting the worst in human nature, but in looking for models that improve upon it.

Adam Smith affirmed Aristotle's skepticism about human nature in politics. Rulers tend to be the "great spendthrifts of society," he observed, "and it is presumptuous of them to pretend to watch over the economy of private people. Let them, instead, look well after their own expense, and they may safely trust private people with theirs. If their own extravagance does not ruin the state, that of their own subjects never will."

What would Adam Smith do? He had observed that his "butcher" served his own self-interests best when he served the self-interests of his customers. The key, then, to checkmating human nature in government was insistence upon mutual advantage. Thus from two potentially destructive forces would come a positive one. For this insight Adam Smith can be regarded as the precursor of exchange psychology, discussed in essay six.

No less a skeptic was James Madison. He began with the reality that "government is the greatest of all reflections of human nature" and that the one "great difficulty" was to "oblige government to control itself." But like Aristotle and Adam Smith, Madison thought positively about how to do that. "It consists," he explained, "in giving to those who administer each department the necessary constitutional means and personal motives to resist encroachments of the others. The provision for defence must in this, as in all other cases, be made commensurate to the danger of attack. Ambition must be made to counteract ambition. The interests of the man must be with the constitutional rights of the place. It may be a reflection on human nature that such devices should be necessary to control the abuses of government. But ... if men were angels no government would be necessary."

In this essay I take my cue directly from Madison and indirectly from Aristotle and Adam Smith. My own skeptical sense tells me that the answer to Congress's fiscal excesses is to extend to ordinary citizens outside government the same protections Madison provided departments inside, to find a more effective way to allow their fiscal ambitions to counteract those of the professional politicians in Congress. And by "ordinary" citizens I mean those who, as Senator Gramm so aptly put it, "pull the wagon." We hear a lot from those who keep loading the wagon, but very little from those who have to pull it.

THE CRITICAL NEED FOR FISCAL DEMOCRACY

There was a time in our political history when one could count on congressional elections as the people's "referendum," their chance to voice their fiscal, and other, concerns. No more. Congressional elections are now mere rituals, with outcomes 98 percent certain. The great power of the incumbency, and the great power of Political Action Committees to bankroll their favorites back into office and keep challengers out, diminishes democracy in ways we have not yet dared imagine. Congress is no longer a popularly elected body, except in a legalistic sense. It is better thought of as a tenured monopoly, made so by its members' skillful use of public resources to stay in public office.

The idea I suggest, then, is that it is time to bring fiscal "glasnost" to Congress. I envision a new set of fiscal relationships between the members and their constituents, and with two things in mind: to place those relationships on the side of fiscal responsibility and to allow the ambitions of ordinary citizens to counteract the fiscal excesses of the members. The evidence, both historical and psychological, seems clear: Fiscal affairs are simply too important to be trusted exclusively any longer to those who profit politically by profligacy. The way out is to reorder their human relations with those who have to "pull the wagon" by giving the pullers genuine voice about what goes into "the wagon" and how to pay for it.

KNUT WICKSELL ON FISCAL DEMOCRACY

In 1896, when the Swedish economist Knut Wicksell set forth a "new principle" for tax fairness, he affirmed an old one about human behavior: The way decisions are arrived at is as important as the decisions themselves. If the human process is right, the end result will likely be, too. Refusing to make tax fairness a political issue, Wicksell did not let himself get embroiled in end results, like who should pay the most tax and who the least. Instead, he made it a democratic issue. He asserted that the end result will be more fair if all who pay have an equal say. So it was his deep faith in democracy that caused him to assert, as in the quotation at the beginning of this essay, that "no measure should be carried out unless it has the prior unanimous consent or at any rate overwhelming support of the people."[1] For practical purposes Wicksell conceded that getting "unanimous" consent for any tax proposal would be impossible, but he would not budge on the need for at least "overwhelming support."

Wicksell's principle stands in sharp contrast to Congress's current fiscal practices. It borrows "on the quiet" first and then works itself into a partisan lather over who should pay for it. All wrong, Wicksell would have said. Turn the process around: Argue fiscal questions out with the people first, until it is clear what they are willing to pay for. That is the democratic way. Otherwise, fiscal policy simply follows the old rule about "Everything for the people, but nothing by the people."[2]

To illustrate his point, Wicksell imagined how a benevolent, but absolute, ruler would organize taxing and spending. If one were to remove a few century-old archaic words and phrases from Wicksell's description one would be inclined to think that it was today's Congress that the Swedish economist was talking about:

> He [the benevolent despot] would find himself in possession of certain traditional revenues from demesnes, monopolies, imposts and taxes. He would spend this income on the satisfaction of public wants. . . . As regards the distribution of the public burden . . . our ruler would probably not worry overmuch about the thorny question whether the activities of the State adequately compensate his subjects for their sacrifice. Still less would he worry whether each separate state service so compensates each class of citizens. These problems might be forced on his attention only in extreme cases of violent dissatisfaction among all or parts of his people. In general the benevolent despot would rest content when he had collected the public income from the separate classes of property owners and had allocated it to the various public expenditures to the best of his conscience. But since taxes so levied from above are almost bound to seem burdensome to the taxpayer, our ruler would try to avoid the appearance of burdensomeness as best he may. For example, he would give preference to indirect taxation, such as regalia, duties, state enterprises, etc., over direct taxations; he would use fees and dues rather than tax revenues to cover the costs of those state services which are directly demanded by individuals. If the ruler thereby succeeded in increasing public

revenue and expenditure on the quiet, that is if the imposts, dues and fees were not considered as taxes by the people, he would probably congratulate himself on having combined such prosperous finances with so slight a [visible] tax pressure.[3]

HOW DO DEMOCRACY'S "RULERS" MEASURE UP?

Should the reader wish to test how his or her representatives in Washington measure up to Wicksell's "overwhelming support" principle, the following questions may reveal the answer. In offering these questions I assume that the reader's House and Senate members, like my own, "keep in touch" in a variety of ways. They write letters and send printed newsletters to constituents. They write newspaper columns and give radio and TV reports. They hold press conferences. They hold office hours in district or state offices. And they travel about giving speeches and "pressing the flesh" at this event and that.

Now, when speaking of fiscal affairs, do they:

Reveal the cost of government programs?
Tell constituents the cost to each of them personally?
Reveal the price tag of new expenditures before voting for them, so citizens can decide if these expenditures are "worth it"?
Explain who is helped and who hurt by expenditures?
Ask whether raising the debt ceiling is a good or bad idea before doing it?
Offer to send constituents cost-benefit studies of programs they previously voted for?
Agree to refund taxes for failed programs?
Agree to cut programs that no longer fill the need?
Tell constituents how much each owes on the national debt?
Tell how much their own votes have added to the national debt?
Agree to eliminate the fiscal illusions from public finance?
Offer to extend to constituents the same franking privilege that the members of Congress enjoy, so they can "talk back" free?

Questions like these reveal how far the fiscal affairs of Congress are from Wicksell's ideal. They also make clear how badly these fiscal affairs compare with those in the free marketplace. If merchants were to conduct their fiscal affairs in the same secretive manner they would not only be driven out of business; they would be in court defending themselves against charges of acting in restraint of trade. And it may be for this reason that many citizens are confused and cynical about Congress. They expect at least as good treatment as they get in the shopping mall, and they simply are not getting it.

A SOCIOLOGICAL PERSPECTIVE

How is Congress's fiscal behavior to be explained? It is best understood, I believe, as a part of a larger drift of power in our society away from little people to large corporate entities. In gathering increasing fiscal power unto itself Congress is simply following a social trend. What forces are driving this drift toward centralized power and whether little people can ever reverse it become, therefore, fundamental questions.

In a series of perceptive essays, sociologist James Coleman dealt with these questions as they affect the relations between individuals, on the one hand, and what he called "corporate actors," like corporations, conglomerates, trade unions, associations, and, of course, government, on the other. "The question of how they can be under the control of persons becomes an important one," Coleman affirmed. "The dilemma is a serious one: If a corporate actor is too extensively restrained by the wills of natural persons from whom its resources originally came, then it cannot exercise its power toward the outside; if it is insufficiently constrained by these persons, it can use its resources against them, exercising its power to subvert their purposes."[4] Coleman put the political question this way: "What kind of a political system in a society would best allow persons to realize their interests, and yet be safe from the dangers of having lost all their individual power to the state?"

In one of the essays, Coleman focused on the process of concentration and dispersal of power in social systems. In it he inquired "into the process through which corporate actors gain power from persons in society, and the processes by which persons retrieve some of that power."[5]

Coleman began by making a distinction between what he called "benefit" and "usage" rights. "It is often true," he pointed out, "that those who wield corporate power are insulated from the demands of desires of the members or owners. In principle the members have a voice in determining corporate action, but in practice the voice is ineffective and the corporate body is controlled by its managers." And the reason is that the power of the corporation has been split. The managers have usage rights, "the power to determine the specific uses of the corporation's wealth." But the owners hold only the right to "benefit from that use," and "thus their inability to collect together sufficient power to counteract or constrain the power held by the corporation."

What is the result of splitting "usage" and "benefits" rights? It is that "usage rights and benefit rights are in different hands: The usage rights are increasingly in the hands of corporate bodies, with the benefit rights remaining in the hands of individual persons. The result is a population that is increasingly alienated from direct control over their resources, increasingly supported by a set of corporate bodies in whom they have vested that direct control."[6]

What are the prospects of little people reclaiming some of the power captured by corporate actors? Coleman was not sanguine. This shift in power "may be inevitable," he conceded, "as a consequence of the increasing interdependence of persons, and the necessity to delegate many actions to corporate bodies in which events affecting many persons are decided by some collective decision mechanism. The central activities of the society can be seen more and more to be controlled by intangible corporate actors."[7]

But if Coleman was not optimistic about change, he was very clear about the psychological consequence for individuals:

> If the discussion above is valid, the degree to which men feel a sense of control over those activities and events whose outcomes are of interest to them should be a function of two elements: The degree to which his interests are confined to those activities close at hand, and his actual control over various activities. In particular, those persons who have a high degree of interest in events controlled by large corporate bodies should have a lower sense of control than those with interest in events controlled by smaller, more localized corporate bodies (family, neighborhood, etc.). Further, if we assume that the persons' general level of satisfaction derive from their feeling of control over those events that are of interest to them, we should find that the lowest levels of satisfaction are to be found among those whose interests are most far flung.[8]

Coleman's insights define quite precisely both the problem and the challenge of opening up the fiscal affairs of Congress to citizens. The odds are against it: The members hold the "usage" rights, while we have only the "benefit" rights. But as I said, that does not mean we should not try to recapture some lost control. We must try. But how?

First, we must try with our minds. We need a solid intellectual understanding of the role of the individual in a fiscal democracy and of his or her rightful claim on those who govern. The following are six propositions that assert that claim with respect to the affairs of a state, whether fiscal or any other.

THE INTELLECTUAL FOUNDATIONS OF FISCAL DEMOCRACY: SIX PROPOSITIONS

Individual Persons Are Democracy's Greatest and Ultimately Only Resource

Democracy's strength has frequently been assigned elsewhere, to our institutions, our markets and enterprise, our social rules and constitution. These, however, are but projections of the way we are as individuals.

The real test of democracy, then, is how it uses its greatest, ultimate resource. If it fails individuals, it fails itself. It drifts toward absolutism and hollow ritual. The answer to democracy's problems is not less democracy, but more. Always more.

Decisive Actions in a Democratic State Should Be Taken Only When an Overwhelming Majority of the Individuals in It Are in Agreement

Wicksell went right to the heart of the matter. Government by the few is for the few; government by the many is for the many. Any method of decision making that does not involve the many discriminates against the many. Every single person in democracy has not only a right to express his opinions on matters affecting his welfare; he has a right to have a state that helps provide accurate information for doing that.

Ultimate Test of Democracy's Representatives Is Whether They Consult Fully, Openly, and Honestly with Citizens Before Taking Decisive Actions

It is clear that in respect to fiscal affairs most of our representatives have failed that test. Fiscal democracy will dawn the day that they see their main business as not in making political deals with our money, but in making democracy work.

All Individuals Must Have Equal Access to Political Influence

This is not to say that each must get his or her own way; most citizens know that. It does say, however, that if the democratic process is allowed to work, the end result will be better than if it is not. Decisions by all the people are more apt to be for all the people. And that means equal access to influence.

Human Nature Is Best Constrained by a
Requirement for Mutual Advantage

The psychology of human exchange, discussed in essay six, has a powerful message for the operation of fiscal affairs. As perceived now by many citizens, fiscal relations with government are a no-win situation, an unequal exchange. So they must be credited with being rational when they walk out of the political process. Will they come back? Not until they see a genuine chance to have a mutually advantageous exchange.

Long-term Solutions to Democratic Problems
Lie Not in Rigging the Outcomes, but in
Improving the Rules of the Game

One does not improve a sport by tampering with the score. Instead, one works to improve the rules by which the game is played. I assert this proposition because current proposals for balancing the budget, it seems to me, seek to enforce an end result, rather than improving the system that produces those results.

Three current proposals illustrate the point. The proposal for a constitutional amendment to require a balanced budget seeks to enforce that result by mandate. It, in effect, gives up on the democratic process and resorts to a constitutional club. The proposal to give the president a line-item veto is in the same end-result frame. Rather than making the fiscal system more democratic, it gives the chief executive a hammer to pound it into shape. Finally, the proposal to limit the terms of representatives and senators assumes in advance of their elections that they cannot be trusted, so cut the terms of the wastrels short.

My appeal for giving ordinary people a greater voice in fiscal affairs as a way of managing the debt problem takes an opposite path. It extends, rather than curtails, democracy. It would "up" the power of the people to couneract that of elected officials, when they so choose. Perhaps the wisest thing that Knut Wicksell said was this: "There can be justice only among equals." When the strength of the people's voice equals that of Congress we will have fiscal justice.

A LETTER TO MY CONGRESSMAN

I close with a letter to my congressman. In it I try to sum up both the spirit and practice of fiscal democracy. It is also an invitation to other citizens to try their hands at a similar letter to their own representative(s), should they find merit in what I say.

Dear Bob,

Regarding the national debt, I have decided from now on to let my vote do the talking. It is only one vote, but it is mine, and I want to make the most of it. So here are my rules for deciding how I will vote in congressional elections in the future. You will have my vote *if* you:

1. *Stop borrowing now.* In other words, "stop the bleeding." I am not asking you to pay off the debt now, just quit making it worse. That in itself might help the economy enough so that we could start paying off the principal later.

2. *Attach a tax bill to each new spending bill.* When Woodrow Wilson said that spending without taxing was as bad as "taxation without representation" he was right. If you are not willing to stand up and defend a tax *now* it probably is not worth having *now*.

3. *Tell me what proposed new expenditures will cost me personally, and before you vote for them.* Then I can make a citizen's judgment about whether they are worth it. Let's fact it, Bob: In the past you have been less than forthright on such matters. You never explain or defend expenditures. You never mention costs. Instead, I'd like you to treat me like a responsible merchant does. Explain your "product," tell me what it will cost, and promise to stand behind it. Then we will have a basis for achieving mutual satisfaction, the only kind worth having.

4. *Give me a costless and easy way to "talk back."* How about a "citizen's frank," so that I can communicate with you without charge, just as you do with me? It isn't so much the cost of the stamp and envelope as the principle of the thing. "Keeping in touch" is a two-way deal, especially when money is involved. And, oh, about paying for my frank, maybe if you communicated a little less about all those good things you do for me, the cost would even out. That way neither of us could be charged with adding to the national debt.

Well, there they are, Bob, the four conditions for getting my vote. I realize they are unconventional, probably real tough for you to do, too. But all I'm asking, really, is that before spending any more of my hard-earned money you please explain what for, why you think it is needed, and what it will cost me. Then I will tell you if I think it's worth it. In other words, I think the fiscal monkey ought to be on your back, not mine.

Now I know we won't always agree and you have lots of other opinions to reckon with. But that's representative democracy, and it's your job to sort things out. All I'm saying is that each individual must have a voice in that sorting, especially when it involves his or her own money. Moreover, it's your responsibility to help see that they do.

Some will say, of course, that ordinary folks aren't interested enough to talk back, even if they can do it free. Don't be too sure. They are talking back now by walking out of the political process. But if you start asking them *important* questions like "Are you willing to pay for it?" you will soon find out how interested they really are. And when that happens, democracy will be the stronger for it.

Others may say that what I propose is too much democracy: "Every man for himself, and to heck with everybody else." Don't be too sure of that, either. The American people have always shown remarkable ability to weigh needs beyond themselves and make sensible judgments about them. That is our strength. So the real issue is whether you trust us to exercise that strength. Fiscal democracy is much more than about money. It is an open door to a new and better polity for all of us. Knut Wicksell was not talking just about tax fairness; he was talking human capacities and their fulfillment. That is what fiscal democracy is really all about.

Finally, should you wonder how serious I am, allow me to add a fifth condition. If in response to this letter I receive one of those stock replies from your computer thanking me for "my keen interest and positive suggestions," consider my vote already lost. You see, I think it's time we started a new type of relationship about money matters and a good time to start is right now. I hope, upon thinking it over, you'll agree.

Would a letter in this vein do any "good"? How many would it take to reorder the way human nature currently operates in Congress? Ten thousand? One hundred thousand? A million? I do not know. But of this I am fairly confident, based solely upon the way political psychology works: The debt will dial down only when the voices of those "pulling the wagon" dial up. That is the political reality. That will switch human nature from the side of unbalanced budgets to that of balanced budgets, and perhaps more quickly than anyone might suspect.

Notes

ESSAY 1

1. James Madison, *The Federalist,* No. 51. New York: Heritage Press, 1945, p. 348.

2. Adam Smith, *The Wealth of Nations.* Modern Library Edition, New York: Modern Library, 1937, p. 14.

3. For disciplinary references see selected readings at the end of the book.

ESSAY 2

1. Walter Lippmann, *A Preface to Politics.* Ann Arbor: University of Michigan Press, 1962.

2. See *The Four Socratic Dialogues of Plato.* Translated by Benjamin Jouett, Oxford: Clarendon Press, 1903.

3. Aristotle, *Aristotle's Politics.* New York: Modern Library, 1943.

4. Machiavelli, *The Prince.* London: Oxford University Press, 1935.

5. Thomas Hobbes, *The Leviathan.* Oxford: Oxford University Press, 1960.

6. John Locke, *Two Treatises of Government.* Cambridge: Cambridge University Press, 1967.

7. Jean-Jacques Rousseau, *Confessions.* London: J. M. Dent and Sons, 1931. See also *Of the Social Contract.* New York: Harper & Row, 1984.

8. Jeremy Bentham, *Principles of Morals and Legislation.* Oxford: B. Blackwell, 1948.

9. Graham Wallas, *Human Nature in Politics.* London: Constable and Company, 1948.

10. Ibid., p. 15.

11. Lippmann, *A Preface to Politics,* p. 59.

12. Ibid., p. 62.

13. Ibid., p. 63.

14. Ibid., p. 91.

15. Ibid., p. 91.

ESSAY 3

1. For an insightful essay on the fiscal sociology of the public household see Daniel Bell, "The Public Household and the Liberal Society," *The Public Interest* 37 (Fall 1974): pp. 29–68.

2. Aristotle, *Aristotle's Politics*. New York: Modern Library, 1943.

3. Adam Smith, *The Wealth of Nations*. Modern Library Edition, New York: Modern Library, 1937.

4. John Maynard Keynes, *A General Theory of Employment, Interest, and Money*. New York: Macmillan, 1936.

5. Aristotle, *Aristotle's Politics*, p. 55.

6. Smith, *The Wealth of Nations*, p. 329.

7. Ibid.

8. Ibid., p. 878.

9. For a cogent discussion of Keynes's erroneous political assumptions see James M. Buchanan, *The Consequences of Mr. Keynes*. London: Institute of Economic Affairs, Hobart Paper, No. 78, 1978.

10. Sir Ray Harrod, *Life of John Maynard Keynes*. New York: Macmillan, 1951, p. 93.

11. F. A. Hayek, *A Tiger by the Tail: The Keynesian Legacy of Inflation*. London: Hobart Paperback, IEA, 1972, pp. 103–4.

ESSAY 4

1. Robert Merton, *Social Theory and Social Structure*. New York: Free Press, 1968, pp. 61–64.

2. Abraham H. Maslow, *Motivation and Personality*. New York: Harper & Row, 1970, Chapter 4, pp. 35–58.

3. Arthur F. Bentley, *The Process of Government*. Bloomington, Ind.: Principia Press, 1949. (Reprint of 1908 edition.)

4. Max Weber, *From Max Weber: Essays in Sociology*. Translated and edited by H. H. Gerth and C. Wright Mills, New York: Oxford University Press, 1958, p. 78.

5. Ibid., p. 115.

6. Ibid., p. 78.

7. James D. Barber, *The Lawmakers*. New Haven: Yale University Press, 1965.

8. Ibid., p. 224.

9. Ibid., pp. 224–25.

10. Rufus P. Browning and Herbert Jacob, "Power, Motivation and Political Personalities," *Public Opinion Quarterly* 28 (Spring 1964), pp. 75–90.

11. Ibid., p. 90.

12. James L. Payne et al., *The Motivations of Politicians*. Chicago: Nelson-Hall, 1984.

13. Ibid., p. 6.

14. Ibid., p. 175.

15. Ibid., p. 176.

16. Ibid., p. 178.

17. Harold D. Lasswell, *Psychopathology and Politics*. New York: Viking Press, 1930.

18. Harold D. Lasswell, *Power and Personality*. New York: W. W. Norton, 1948.

19. Harold D. Lasswell, *Politics: Who Gets What, When and How*. New York: Peter Smith, 1950.

20. Ibid., p. 16.

21. Ibid., p. 17.

22. Weber, *From Max Weber*, p. 84.

23. Joseph A. Schumpeter, *Capitalism, Socialism and Democracy*. New York: Harper & Brothers, 1942, p. 285.

24. David R. Mayhew, *Congress: The Electoral Connection*. New Haven: Yale University Press, 1974.

25. Ibid., pp. 5–6.

26. Ibid., p. 49.

27. Ibid., pp. 52–53.

28. Ibid., p. 61.

ESSAY 5

1. James S. Coleman, *Individual Interests and Collective Action*. Cambridge: Cambridge University Press, 1986, pp. 163–91.

ESSAY 6

1. Sidney R. Waldman, *The Foundations of Political Action: An Exchange Theory of Politics*. Boston: Little Brown, 1972, p. 7.

2. Ibid., p. 7.

3. Waldman offers a different set of propositions from my own (pp. 22–23), but the reader will note similarities, too:

> (1) If in the past the occurrence of a stimulus or set of stimuli has been the occasion on which a man's activity has been rewarded, then the more similar the present stimulus situation is to the past one, the more likely he is to perform the activity, or some similar activity, now.
>
> (2) The more often within a given period a man's activity rewards the activity of another, the more often the other will perform that activity.
>
> (3) The more valuable to a man a unit of activity another gives him, the more often he will perform the activity rewarded by that activity of the other.
>
> (4) The more often in the recent past a man has received a rewarding activity from another, the less valuable any further units of that activity become to him.
>
> (5) The more to a man's disadvantage the rule of distributive justice fails of realization, the more likely he is to display anger and, in anger, the results of aggressive behavior are rewarding.

4. The following historical references are from Lewis Kimmel, *Federal Budget and Fiscal Policy, 1789–1958*. Washington, D.C.: Brookings Institution, 1959. See Chapters 1 and 2, pp. 7–98.

5. For a thoughtful analysis of this subject, see Robert E. Lane, "Market Justice and Political Justice," *American Political Science Review* 80, No. 2 (June

1986). Lane examines why a "sense of controlling one's own destiny in the market, but not in politics, leads to more of a sense of political injustice than market injustice."

ESSAY 7

1. *The Bible*, Job 1:1.

2. Joseph A. Schumpeter, *Capitalism, Socialism and Democracy*. New York: Harper and Brothers, 1942, p. 269.

3. Ibid., see Chapter 22, "Another Theory of Democracy," pp. 269–83, and Chapter 23, "The Inference," pp. 284–302.

4. James McGregor Burns, *Congress on Trial*. New York: Harper and Brothers, 1949, p. 19.

5. Anthony Downs, *An Economic Theory of Democracy*. New York: Harper and Brothers, 1957, p. 8.

6. James Madison, *The Federalist,* No. 51. New York: Heritage Press, 1945, p. 348.

ESSAY 8

1. *Congressional Record.* January 31, 1985, H302.

2. For a good discussion of this, see Steven H. Haeberle, "The Institutionalization of the Subcommittee in the United States House of Representatives," *The Journal of Politics* 40 (1978), pp. 1054–65.

3. Vilfredo Pareto, *Cours d'Economie Politieque,* in *Sociological Writings.* Selected and introduced by S. E. Finer, New York: Frederick F. Praeger, 1966.

4. Arthur Burns, *AEI Economist,* April 1979, p. 5.

5. For perceptive discussions of fiscal illusion see James M. Buchanan, *Public Finance in Democratic Process*. Chapel Hill: The University of North Carolina Press, 1967, pp. 89, 126–43; and James M. Buchanan (with Richard E. Wagner), *Democracy in Deficit*. New York: Academic Press, 1977, pp. 128–30, 138.

6. See James M. Buchanan, "Puviani and the Fiscal Illusion," in *Fiscal Theory and Political Economy*. Chapel Hill: University of North Carolina Press, 1960, pp. 59-64.

7. Ibid., p. 61.

8. Quoted from Report of the Committee on the Judiciary, United States Senate, Ninety-seventh Congress, First Session, March 11, 1981, p. 21.

ESSAY 9

1. *Hearings before the Subcommittee on the Constitution,* Ninety-seventh Congress, First Session, on S.J. 9, S.J. Res. 43, and S.J. Res. 58, March 11, April 9, May 20, 1981, p. 30.

2. F. A. Hayek, "Whither Democracy?" in *New Studies*. London: Routledge and Kegan Paul, 1978, pp. 152–62.

3. Bertrand de Jouvenel, *The Ethics of Redistribution*. Cambridge: Cambridge University Press, 1952.

4. Ibid., p. 74.

ESSAY 10

1. *Congressional Record* (hereafter *CR*), October 9, 1985, S 12961.
2. *CR*, October 31, 1985, S 12572–73.
3. Ibid., H 9556.
4. *CR*, October 23, 1985, H 9067.
5. *CR*, October 30, 1985, H 9437.
6. *CR*, October 22, 1985, H 8993.
7. *CR*, November 13, 1987, S 16264.
8. *CR*, November 4, 1985, S 14717.
9. *CR*, January 3, 1985, S 334.
10. *CR*, October 9, 1985, S 12961.
11. Ibid., S12973.
12. Ibid., S 12972.
13. *CR*, October 4, 1985, S 12629.
14. *CR*, October 30, 1985, H 9451.
15. Ibid., H 9438.
16. *CR*, October 9, 1985, S 12965.
17. *CR*, January 3, 1985, S 17–18.
18. *CR*, October 9, 1985, S 12963.
19. *CR*, November 13, 1987, S 16248.
20. *CR*, October 30, 1985, H 9453.
21. *CR*, October 3, 1985, S 12570, and September 25, 1985, S 12084.
22. *CR*, October 4, 1985, S 12641.

ESSAY 11

1. See Jawaharlal Nehru, *The Discovery of India*. New York: John Day Company, 1946, and *An Autobiography*. London: John Lane, 1936.

ESSAY 12

1. Adam Smith, *The Wealth of Nations*. New York: Modern Library, 1937, p. 882.

ESSAY 13

1. James M. Buchanan, *Liberty, Market, and State*. Brighton, Sussex: Wheatsheaf Books, 1986, p. 216.

ESSAY 14

1. Knut Wicksell, "A New Principle of Just Taxation," in Richard A. Musgrave and Alan T. Peacock, Editors, *Classics in the Theory of Public Finance*. New York: Macmillan, 1958, pp. 72–118.
2. Ibid., p. 109.
3. Ibid., p. 83.

4. James S. Coleman, *Individual Interests and Collective Action*. Cambridge: Cambridge University Press, 1986.

5. Ibid., pp. 267–80.

6. Ibid., p. 270.

7. Ibid., p. 271.

8. Ibid., p. 273.

Selected Readings

Only a few of the following bibliographic sources speak directly to the causal connection between human nature on the one hand and Congress and the debt on the other. The paucity of such linking literature testifies to the need for research on the subject. As conceptual foundations, however, these references are invaluable. Each in its own unique way contributes to the intellectual stock from which a coherent political psychology of the debt will eventually come.

Barner-Barry, Carol, and Robert Rosenwein. *Psychological Perspectives on Politics*. Englewood Cliffs, N.J.: Prentice-Hall, 1985. The authors show what the psychological approach to the study of politics has to offer. They assume that psychological insights complement rather than supplement those found in related fields such as anthropology, sociology, economics, and history.

Buchanan, James M. *The Calculus of Consent*. (With Gordon Tullock.) Ann Arbor: University of Michigan Press, 1962.

____. *Democracy in Deficit*. (With Richard E. Wagner.) New York: Academic Press, 1977.

____. *Fiscal Responsibility in Constitutional Democracy*. (With Richard E. Wagner.) Boston: Marainus A, 1978.

____. *Liberty, Market, and State*. Brighton, Sussex: Wheatsheaf Books, 1986.

____. *Public Financing in Democratic Process*. Chapel Hill: University of North Carolina Press, 1967. The works of this Nobel Laureate (Economics) in the field of public debt are both extensive and comprehensive and filled with political/psychological insights. Must reading for considering the human factor in the debt.

Cantril, Hadley. "Some Requirements for a Political Psychology," in Malcom B. Parsons, Ed., *Perspectives in the Study of Politics*. Chicago: Rand McNally, 1968. Transactional psychology is the basis for the listed requirements.

Coleman, James S. *Individual Interests and Collective Action*. Cambridge: Cambridge University Press, 1986. Part II on power provides an excellent theoretic framework for understanding deficit spending as political power.

Davis, James C. *Human Nature in Politics*. New York: John Wiley & Sons, 1963. The author conducts a search of the origins of political behavior.

Deutch, Morton. "What Is Political Psychology?" *International Social Science Journal* 35 (1983), pp. 221–36. A useful overview of the field, including historical development, content, and applications.

DiRenzo, Gordon J. *Personality, Power, and Politics*. Notre Dame: University of Notre Dame Press, 1967. This book is remarkable for both its content and its array of relevant references.

Downs, Anthony. *An Economic Theory of Democracy*. New York: Harper and Brothers, 1957. Downs's hypothesis is that "governments continue spending until the marginal vote gain from expenditure equals the marginal vote loss from financing." The author's development of this hypothesis yields a number of insights into political behavior.

Eulau, Heinz. *The Behavioral Persuasion in Politics*. New York: Random House, 1967. "Why do people behave politically as they do?" is the subject of inquiry. The author finds that "it is because their behavior satisfies personal needs, demands, and drives, or because it releases tensions and frustrations, or because it compensates for deprivations, or because it reveals private perceptions and values."

Federalist, The. New York: Heritage Press, 1945. The papers by James Madison, and especially No. 51, provide the democratic rationale for reckoning both realistically and constructively with the problem of human nature in government.

Fiorina, Morris P. *Congress: Keystone of the Washington Establishment*. New Haven: Yale University Press, 1977. The political insights are far-ranging and thought-provoking. The "Alternative Views" presented at the end leave the reader to choose.

_____. "The Decline of Collective Responsibility in American Politics." *Daedalus* 109 (Summer 1980), pp. 25–45. Fiorina contends that the "modern age demands . . . that we worry about our ability to make government work *for* us. The problem is that we are gradually losing that ability, and a principal reason for this loss is the steady erosion of *responsibility* in American politics."

Fitzgerald, Ross. "Human Needs and Politics: The Ideas of Christian Bay and Herbert Marcuse." *Political Psychology* 6, No. 1 (1985). The article demonstrates how the idea of "human needs is crucial to the political theory of Bay and Marcuse."

Freedman, Ann E., and P. E. Freedman. *The Psychology of Political Control*. New York: St. Martin's Press, 1975. "How do the rulers control the ruled?" is the question pursued. The authors show how knowledge of contemporary psychology can be applied fruitfully to the political realm.

Greenstein, Fred I. *Personality and Politics*. New York: W. W. Norton and Company, 1969. A careful analysis of how personality characteristics do, and do not, help to explain political behavior.

Hayek, F. A. "Whither Democracy?" in *New Studies*. London: Routledge and Kegan Paul, 1978, pp. 152–62. "The root of the trouble," Hayek asserts, "is that so-called 'legislatures' . . . have become omnipotent governmental bodies."

Hermann, Margaret G., Ed. *Political Psychology*. San Francisco: Jossey-Bass, 1986. The editor's prologue: "What Is Political Psychology?" speaks to the tenets and issues of political psychology, as do the selections in the book.

Homans, George Caspar. *Social Behavior*. New York: Harcourt Brace Jovanovich, 1974. The author's "general propositions," stated in Chapter 2, provide a theoretic underpinning for understanding the social behavior called deficit spending behavior.

Jacobson, Gary C. *The Politics of Congressional Elections*. Boston: Little Brown, 1983. In Chapter 7 Jacobson points out how congressional office is an "individual franchise" that may work against the "collective good."

Kirkpatrick, Samuel A., and Pettit, Lawerence K. *The Social Psychology of Political Life*. Belmont, Cal.: Duxbury Press, 1972. A wide-ranging anthology of 26 works under such titles as "Personality Attributes," "The Psycho-Cultural Context of Politics," "Political Perception," and "Political Motivation."

Knutson, Jeanne N., General Ed. *Handbook of Political Psychology*. San Francisco: Jossey-Bass, 1973. A collection of 16 articles demonstrates quite graphically the interdisciplinary nature of the subject.

____. *The Human Basis of the Polity, a Psychological Study of Political Men*. Chicago: Aldine, Atherton, 1972. This book provides an assessment of previous political psychology and an agenda for future research.

Lane, Robert E. "Market Justice and Political Justice." *American Political Science Review* 80, No. 2 (June 1986), pp. 383–402. Must reading for anyone interested in the differences between justice in the market and politics. Implications for deficit spending are direct and real.

____. *Political Life: Why People Get Involved in Politics*. Glencoe, Ill.: Free Press, 1959. A good exposition of the limitations of psychological forces in political analysis.

Lasswell, Harold D. *Politics: Who Gets What, When and How*. New York: Peter Smith, 1950.

____. *Power and Personality*. New York: W. W. Norton, 1948.

____. *Psychopathology and Politics*. New York: Viking Press, 1962. Lasswell's key hypothesis about the power seeker is that he pursues power as a means of compensating for deprivation.

Laver, Michael. *The Politics of Private Desires*. Middlesex, England: Penguin Books, 1981. This book is about the political consequences of private desires. It is based on the assumption that people participate in politics in order to further their own private objectives.

Lippmann, Walter. *A Preface to Politics*. Ann Arbor: University of Michigan Press, 1962. Probably the best popular treatment of human nature in politics. Lippmann regarded human beings as the real "center" for political thought.

Maslow, Abraham H. *Motivation and Personality*. New York: Harper & Row, 1970. An understanding of motivational needs, here set forth in a hierarchical order, is basic to perceptions about why members of Congress prefer deficit spending to taxing.

Mayhew, David R. *Congress: The Electoral Connection*. New Haven: Yale University Press, 1974. A classic, this small volume is concerned with what public officials actually do. It does not assume that "officials will automatically translate policy into law once somebody finds out what it is."

Merriam, Charles E. *New Aspects of Politics*. Chicago: University of Chicago Press, 1925. This early work in political science is historically notable, and especially for Chapter 4: "Politics and Psychology." Merriam opened with these lines:

"The friendship between politics and psychology is an old one. Politicians have always been rule-of-thumb psychologists, and some psychologists have understood the art of politics. Between the developing science of psychology and the newer politics, the relationship is likely to become even more intimate in the future than in the past."

Payne, James L., et al. *The Motivations of Politicians*. Chicago: Nelson-Hall, 1984. This study is a stimulating attempt to formulate a typology for use in analyzing the motivations of individual politicians.

Rivers, A. H. R. *Psychology and Politics, and Other Essays*. London: Kegan Paul. French Trubner, 1923. The value of this essay is historical. It was written at a time when, as the author put it, "the science of psychology is still very young" and when "we all recognize that the art of government is far more than a matter ruled by intellect."

Schumpeter, Joseph. *Capitalism, Socialism and Democracy*. New York: Harper and Brothers, 1942. The formidable title should not turn off those interested in political psychology. The skepticism of this economist of the Austrian School leapfrogs cynicism and provides positive insights. An example is section three of Chapter 22: "Human Nature in Politics."

Simon, Herbert A. "Human Nature in Politics: The Dialogue of Psychology with Political Science." *The American Political Science Review* 79 (1985), pp. 293–304. The author offers a commentary on the role of the rationality principle in recent political science research.

Stone, William F., and David C. Smith. "Human Nature in Politics." *Political Psychology* 4, No. 4 (1983), pp. 693–711. This article traces the development of Graham Wallas's thought and examines important intellectual influences on him.

Waldman, Sidney R. *The Foundations of Political Action: An Exchange Theory of Politics*. Boston: Little Brown, 1972. Waldman presents an exchange theory of politics and uses "the framework of learning psychology to suggest how reinforcement conditions human behavior as men try to increase rewards and reduce costs."

Wallas, Graham. *Human Nature in Politics*. London: Constable and Company, 1948. This pioneering work in political psychology rambles but is brilliant in its human insights. Chapter 3, "Non-rational Inference in Politics," places political activity squarely in human nature's camp.

Weber, Max. "Politics as a Vocation." In H. H. Gerth and C. Wright Mills, Eds. *From Max Weber: Essays in Sociology*. New York: Oxford University Press, 1958. Politics for Weber meant "striving to share power or striving to influence the distribution of power either among states or among groups of states."

Weldon, T. D. *States and Morals*. New York: Whittlesey House, McGraw-Hill, 1947. The following statement sets the tone for this tightly written philosophic book on political ethics: "Rulers . . . since they are human, are only too likely to become a vested interest unless steps are taken to prevent them from doing so; and it is therefore expedient to prevent too much strength from being concentrated in any one person or body."

Index

About the Author

COLE S. BREMBECK is Professor and Associate Dean for International Studies, emeritus, Michigan State University. His interest in political psychology began early because his father was a state legislator and holder of other elective offices. At the University of Wisconsin he majored in communication with concentrations in political communication and classical rhetoric. His Ph.D. dissertation examined the psychology of political persuasion. In his role as Associate Dean for International Studies he had the opportunity over an extended period to observe political psychology at work not only domestically in Washington, but also globally in a number of foreign countries.